il cuore : the heart

_____

WESLEYAN POETRY

Also by Kathleen Fraser

POETRY
Change of Address 1966
In Defiance (of the Rains) 1969
Little Notes to You from Lucas Street 1972
What I Want 1974
Magritte Series 1977
New Shoes 1978
Each Next 1980
Something (even human voices) in the foreground, a lake 1984
boundayr (Limited edition, with aquatints by Sam Francis) 1987
Notes preceding trust 1987
from a text (Limited edition, with paintings by Mary Ann Hayden) 1993
when new time folds up 1993
WING (Limited edition) 1995

FOR CHILDREN
Stilts, Somersaults and Headstands 1968

AUDIO (Poetry)
Even human voices 1986

VIDEO (Anthology)
Women Working in Literature 1992

il cuore : the heart

Selected Poems 1970–1995

❖

K A T H L E E N   F R A S E R

Introduction by Peter Quartermain

Wesleyan University Press
Published by University Press of New England
Hanover and London

Wesleyan University Press
Published by University Press of New England, Hanover, NH 03755
© 1997 by Kathleen Fraser
All rights reserved
Printed in the United States of America
5 4 3 2 1
CIP data appear at the end of the book

A Note on Uncollected Poems

Poems appearing in the final "New and Uncollected" section were originally published in the following journals: "In Commemoration of the Visit of Foreign Commercial Representatives to Japan, 1947," *TEMBLOR* 9; "A Little Background: the Sisters," *Sulfur* 26; "La La at the Cirque Fernando, Paris," *IRONWOOD* 31/32 The Final Issue; "Cue or Starting Point," *The Iowa Review* 26, n. 2; "WING," *Conjunctions*: 24.

   WING also appeared as a limited edition chapbook from EM Press, 1995.

for Arturo and for David

Contents

from *Each Next* narratives [1980]

from *Something (even human voices) in the foreground, a lake* [1984]

from *Notes preceding trust* [1987]

from *when new time folds up* [1993]

New and Uncollected Poems [Selections from 1978–1995]

Introduction

Resistance. According to E. M. Forster in *A Passage to India*, "most of life is so dull that there is nothing to be said about it." How fight that astonishing negative? How extricate oneself from what Kathleen Fraser in a letter called "the assigned identity of others' convenience"? How maintain a vital perturbability, how claim and embrace it in the teeth of definition and its closure? "The accidents / interest me," says Fraser. For her "the purposeful fingers of chance" deliver the flatfootedness and pain of the unexpected, and the wit of error, compelling reminders that you cannot wholly control your life. As the first version of "this. notes. new year." (1980) puts it, "She wanted a 'flow' she thought, but in the translation it was corrected, displacing the *o* and substituting *a* . She could give herself to an accident." Listen to the mistakes; then, heed them (as in *boundayr*). Attend! ("But what does it *mean?*" they ask, seeking the key to all mythologies.)

The necessity to break preprogrammed poetics, to challenge preset forms, has been in Fraser's work pretty well from the start, perhaps even from her grade seven poetry classes, where, she tells us, "what had been joyful became flattened and restrictive," and she learned to hate the frame of mechanized response to guessed-at authorial intent. Her own poetry interrogates the role of the poet in the writing process. Hers is a poetics of discovery; it belongs to no school. In her ground-breaking essay "The Tradition of Marginality" (written in 1985) Fraser talks of "a different kind of attentiveness, . . . a listening attitude, an attending to unconscious connections, a backing off of the ego to allow the mysteries of language to come forward and resonate more fully." As her work progresses, the attention of the poems shifts more and more to the compositional process as a means of undermining the traditional idea of authorial control over the "well-crafted" poem. In her essay on the line (1988) she speaks of disobedience and its necessities—"Breaking rules, breaking boundaries, crossing over, going where you've been told not to go"—as one of the true tasks of the poet. "How she notices," observes a line in "Locations" (1978), "is a formal fact." Innovative, it is a writing that *attests*, driven by abiding curiosity and persistence of vision, listening to the multiple voices clamoring inside her.

Fraser's resistance to consequence derives in part from her sense of the instability, the indeterminacy, the undecidability, of language, and from her constant suspicion that "the scrubbed and well-brushed historic formulas of the known," themselves linguistic constructs, actively prevent us from recognizing the multiple and idiosyncratic by upholding received models of perfection. It derives in part, too, from the apprehension of female *inconsequence* which she contested so innovatively and influentially in *HOW(ever)* (1983–1991). In editing this journal, she radically transformed the notion of consequence by publishing linguistically foregrounded celebrations of the fragmented and "merely domestic" experience of women. It derives in part, too, from three great permission-givers, Barbara Guest, George Oppen, and Wallace Stevens, whose music, accuracy, and attentiveness to words "unloosed" ordinary habits of reading; this developing poetics facilitated Fraser's formal explorations and her development of a voice capable of illuminating women's variousness through an accessible yet *un*common language of personal experience.

Uncommon language is more plainly the hallmark of the recent poems than of the earlier, yet her writing has always been responsive to its own occasion, for Fraser is an astonishingly up-front writer. In work after work her persistent determination to address a subject directly, and with great vulnerability, immediately engages the reader in precariousness, bypassing expected readings, eschewing the conventional. "What I want / oh I want it," the poet sang in "Gloom Song" (1969), "though I don't know / what I want"—a theme elaborated, perhaps, as in the disturbances of "The History of My Feeling" (1971). Speaking directly of the poet's personal life, its passionate and gendered intelligence tells us that

> Last night, pinned by a shaft of pain—
> your presence and your absence—
> I knew clearly that I hated you
> for entering me profoundly, for taking me inside you,
> for husbanding me, claiming all that I knew
> and did not know,
> yet letting me go from you
> into this unpredictable and loneliest of weathers.

Precariousness. Gender. Complicated by a fierce independence, yet a largeness of sympathy and generosity of spirit. How difficult it is, the poem reminds us, simply to cope, in the imperative of resistance. And how hard one is on oneself, faced with broken plates, separated friendships, the ordinariness of one's daily life, the fractures and discontinuities attendant upon feeling and passion. What I want. *Il cuore*.

"The History of My Feeling" reveals Fraser's response to language as agent of discovery: the puns, the handling of consonants, the variation of tempo and line, all further the disclosure of feeling into thought, thought into feeling; the remarkable music carries the attention and lifts an almost prosaic syntax, gesturing toward the later cross-generic moves of *Magritte Series* (1977) and *Each Next* (1980), and more recent work. "Giotto: ARENA" (1992), with its consonant clusters, its play with quantity, its quite wonderful vowel-sequences, its responsiveness to error, develops a remarkable syntax which forwards while yet circling back and incorporates the graphic as a driving and mediating force—enabling the graphic occasion itself to become the spur of writing response:

—— massed ——————————————————————
He masses pale clothed bodies—relieved with beloved and
random Venetian stripes; blue is sparingly ppressedd . . .

.

His own palpate softens theory's sharp folds

seeing lLargE blank surfaces' close-up seeing

Like much of Fraser's recent work, this is a demanding poem, an intense and difficult engagement with history and time, language and culture, falsehood and accuracy, all the stops pulled out.

Given its visual and syntactic innovation, *il cuore : the heart* (a selection that spans twenty-five years) is above all else the work of emotional necessity and indeed spiritual connection. "The limits of language," Fraser has said, "present us, continually, with the limits of what we might know about ourselves." These poems extend what we know, and are an exhilaration.

PETER QUARTERMAIN

from *What I Want* [1974]

Seven Uneasy Songs

1. What I Want

Because you are constantly coming to begin,
I suggest solutions and
am full of holes. See through me
when my back is turned.

A hotel is the notion of entrance
by thought. Your love is

constantly a solution,
criminally full
of no difference
when my back is turned.

I read your thoughts because
you are constantly changing and
coming through me
when my back is turned. And

I want something
for something, constantly.
Coming.

2. To Start

At a tremendous speed my throat makes its door slide.
Open. Pure guesswork . . . I have lost the other

side of me. You'll see. In teeth dreams there are only three
wrong guesses. A surprise doesn't exist.

Just a guess against the door.
To think is simultaneous. I'll take another network

of teeth (by pairs) as my answer. Stars. Anymore.

3. Amid Mouths

More and more
rushes out at night
high on the still pooled joyful "do not."

Blood cells
desert for signs inside me.
A narrow ledge.

The buoyant
with furry necks,
more and more.

.

We are what is
that the rare elegant necks
(more of them)
look attentively at
a baby us.

They peer over the wooden boat
but it is shore
starts
        to roll. Flapping
seaward, the heron ascends

each wing rained thin.

.

That I snap
(but watch the little light)
just open
up
the dark see.

A wonderful move
these very gentle whites
amid mouths.

4. Growing Up

In a box I marry
and grow firm.
I fly to complacency
where hair runs by the ankle.

I pull Mother's dress: "Come down
out of each other's knees!" . . . and and
"fresh lines"   (linen).

Is nothing the strength
of my wings' chain?

.

The grass learned again
how often the body leans
in a clearing

(and another one breaks in on
the pleasure of her stare)

                but it seemed
the time.

.

I just wanted a soft green family.

Remember your family?

My family sadly grow less.

It's more difficult with maps

zipped inside. Show my face

in pink silk. A simple box.

5. Going

Through his giant photo body,
heaven's blue sea.

I am leaving and will close my tongue.

.

To and fro men
(particularly)
grow

windows.
Horizon. In.

.

Trees open in the neck &

his mother's thumb appears in
the lentil heart
flood.

6. If

Suppose we are a fragment,

a perfect night of immediacy
in vital places.

Up here I am the disguised flower
and you are where it came from.

To allow the hidden.
So slowly, my body.

And wouldn't you

begin
to make friends with it?

I can wait.

7. That Didn't

That didn't come down
      but quietly (to touch)
      as wheat grows. And shoes
in water. Here. A curving brown light
didn't drop down all around.
      No center.
      No field where that touch seemed
firm, almost.

[San Francisco, 1972]

Little Notes to You, from Lucas Street

1

In Iris mud
her legs stems
and separate even
if it's afternoon by the porch

2

Still her curls are just unwinding
from the large-size pinks
Plastics fresh as spring
Mud rushes up in her throat

3

There's a song she's trying
to remember she knows
it's there   Her boys are there
on each muddy bike

4

Red paint and blue paint
bicycles   The sun's
the sun's out as a presence
of snow running

5

I don't know
where I am   Bread rises and smells
Only half an inch
of pink detergent and my hands
compose with two oranges

6

Is my mouth a pocket?
Its mystery
a presence as separate as the porch
The children in our puddle
walk reverently
in green and red sweatshirts

7

Somewhere a switch disconnecting
Along the white edge of
snowlight nothing hurts
Call me with your danger

8

Red deep red,
anemones purple anemones
We watch them float
somewhere near the center of the table
Anne is getting married
The petals' dark tensing center

9

Are you the mysterious presence?
One always waits
The possible new thrill
could be licking a stamp

10

Seeing again
The tension stretched so exquisitely pale
it almost disappeared behind love
And the one thing you never tell me

11

Your knees move in spite of you
They reveal the shape
of your face   On the bus
we showed off our children   See,
I can play mommy and daddy

12

Long glossy cars at ease in the parking zones
always gliding through the temporary zones
stopping firmly before the non-stop zones
Their confidence tilts
the only balance one has mastered

[Iowa City, 1970]

The History of My Feeling

for D.

The history of my feeling for you (or is it the way you change
and are blameless like clouds)
$\qquad\qquad$ reminds me of the sky in Portland
and the morning I unpacked
and found the white plates from Iowa City
broken,
$\qquad$ consistently surprising with cracks,
petals like new math theories smashed
$\qquad\qquad\qquad$ with the purposeful fingers of chance.
I loved the plates. They were remnants from an auction
which still goes on in my head because of the auctioneer's body
and his sexy insinuations about the goods he was selling.

But to Ruth, who talked them into their thin wraps of newspaper,
what we were sharing was departure and two lives breaking
and learning
$\qquad$ to mend into new forms.

We had loved our husbands,
$\qquad\qquad$ torn our bodies in classic ways to bear
$\qquad\qquad\qquad$ children: Sammy, David, Wesley—
Now we loved new men and wept together
so that the plates weren't important and hadn't been packed
with the care I might have given had I been alone.
But Ruth was with me.

You were gone, like this storm that's been arriving and
$\qquad\qquad\qquad$ disappearing
all morning.

$\qquad$ I awoke to hear heavy rain in the gutters.
The light was uncertain and my feelings had grown less sure.
Last night, pinned by a shaft of pain—
$\qquad\qquad$ your presence and your absence—
I knew clearly that I hated you
for entering me profoundly, for taking me inside you,
for husbanding me, claiming all that I knew
$\qquad\qquad\qquad$ and did not know,
yet letting me go from you
into this unpredictable and loneliest of weathers.

$\qquad\qquad\qquad$ [1971]

from *New Shoes* [1978]

Six Poems from Magritte Series *[1977]*

La Baigneuse Du Clair Au Sombre

I am floating
in a tub of water
moving toward the lights.

He is floating in the water,
he is wiping the table
with a dirty napkin.

The place is big.
I can feel it breathing.
We are moving toward the lights.

The dream about my death
drops into my head,
foamy red and almost boiling.

I don't want it to happen
if it's going to hurt.
The things I hear

are going out my left ear
and moving
toward the lights

like a woman wearing a red sweater.
Wearing a red sweater,
I am attracted

by the view behind her,
out the window
at the civilized periphery.

It is clean.
It is highly finished
like these clothes of mine

moving toward the lights.
I'm sliding down the bench
into the scenery

out the window
towards the woman.
I'm thinking about inertia

as the wall vanishes.
The woman is dancing.
I am thinking about the woman

sliding toward the lights.
The red sweater vanishes.
Again, the ending gets a little vague,

as she slowly puts her arm
around his shoulder, as she slowly
puts a dagger through the bones

in his chest. She puts lights
in his chest. Her arm is
a big cloak. Pieces of him glow

all over the room.
I recognize nothing
but the color of brown

wrapping paper. Now
she's giving me
the big present.

[1/6/75]

L' Invention Collective

of the marigolds, of blue vinyl suitcase, of crud all over the stove
she'd left shiniest
     two to bring light to,
     yes a shelf in reach where the little both of them could begin
     could make his clean start as fresh as Watermelon slice (oh
     where was her life?)
          in him his tiny mysteries her laughing sound alight
          in his throat

          oh what was a mother to do, being her, and suddenly
                         it's now?

when she went away there was this big boy who pushed him
when she went away they pushed him in the puddle
he was running home, he was running home and she wasn't there

but trying somewhere else to find out who
and where, was she?

        was she not the neat and tidy? did she not see
        her seducers in a line and shaking their fingers and showing
        "be here, be here"

in her mind (was it?) she lay at the edge of the waters, at the
edge of the waters
     was it sand there? was her fish skin bare? all she knows is
     it scratches and when the waves collapse in inches she cannot
     swim for her finny body's half human.   One day she's
     plunk on the shore and her image comes to her   in a picture
     as though holding a mirror of blue paint
       just a whiff of horizon and the little waves creeping
         and folding   and there it is, no way of turning her
         back now   her thighs/knees, softest whirring of
         crotch hair   and all the color of how she ought to be
         but suddenly those fins
         and the beginning of silver slippery fish-lady lying,
         no arms no woman swimming, but a face cut deep with
         gills and the sad eyes panting

and the absolute quiet of something about to arrive.

                                       [4/20/75]

Les Valeurs Personnelles

As a child she'd often considered the bathroom as her future, how it would be if it were her place to be alone in. Under the porcelain sink would be the stove. Next to the toilet, the radio (there was just enough space). She could sleep in the tub. Under it her blanket would be folded. There would be apples. A flashlight. Her mystery books. And no one would come in there, the mess would go away.

Later she chose a boat. It appeared to her in a dream, before rising, and was smoothly crafted in the shape of a canoe but made of many pieces of wood of a natural nut-brown color. Its insides were sleek. She could manage, feeling the lift of the water under her. There was her comb leaning against one side, and a mirror hung just under the seat. It would send out light, little flashes of it, as though there were an electric storm about to approach. And caught in one corner, to maintain the sense of home, a curtain of soft white cotton, as though a window were behind it, to open, if one wanted to look out. For surely, white clouds caught in the precise boundaries of the window's rectangle would give one a different sense of motion, of how long it took a cloud to float from one edge to the other. On the floor of the boat, she imagined an oriental rug, proportioned not to overwhelm the purity of the boat's intention. It fell into character, providing backdrop. Often she would place several objects there—a wooden match with yellow sulphur tip or one of those rich cakes of soap with beveled edge, oval, smelling of apricot, never touched, yet reflected in the mirror in two parts, as if used or broken.

This morning she'd awakened smelling the sea. Before thought, she'd noticed an urgency in her left foot to dangle in the water, and it crept up into her body, pulling, wanting the openness of the sea, the wetness, wanting her body to be taken into the largeness without any walls, no object to distract her into order. She felt the boat tipping. She felt the possibility of doing nothing to stop it.

[8/11/75]

Les Jours Gigantesques

Have you noticed the shadow hovering?
      How when you are in the middle of brushing your teeth
      there is something gathering around the corner?
She is dreaming this thought to a self
awake in the world
when she feels a tug, something like a hand pressing
down upon her thigh
      and she remembers she is naked and alone in the room
      and wishes for her silk blouse
      and the zipper with its three silver hooks at the top.
In her body's emptiness
a growing sense of intimacy,
the pressure of a shadow in its black suit,
its right hand moving
around her waist, as if looking
for a pocket,
      or the push of a head against
      her shoulder, as though
      this movie from some little light booth
      on the opposite wall was focusing,
      on her, and the image was him,
      his half head
moving towards her nipple,
with the thirst in him, dark
against her white body. She looks down,
      she looks down at, oh, the hand, or is it
      the shadow of a hand
      pressing in on the thigh that is hers.
Her muscles bulge with effort
and become tremendous
in their flex. The color drains
from every part of her, but
      the red mouth,
      holding its shape steadily,
      the scream, at first uncertain,
      enters the air
      and becomes the third,
      the knowing, between them.

[8/14/75]

La Reproduction Interdite

for R.M.

I am interested in the logic of secrets, how it has always moved me, in particular, to be invited by a face into the aura of its withholding, as though we were designed to bring forward two opposing sets of facts and bathe ourselves in the resulting struggle, as in watching a tight-rope walker move from one point in space to another, each foot brought precisely from behind and placed in front of the other, but without the delicious possibility of falling, were it not for the rope stretched tautly beneath him, cutting the air with its odor of hemp.

The secrets between men and women are of peculiar fascination. My father, for example, invited me into a dream last summer where I discovered that he was making preparations to die. He was busy doing small errands, rushing about in his impeccably tailored suit and polished shoes, with a face so sad, so preoccupied with its secret, so designed to escape observation that I immediately began to pay attention, invited as I was by that closed-off expression to become the rope upon which he demonstrated his journey.

As I watched him moving to get everything in order before leaving, my sense of dismay began to take on its own life, expanding into anger and then curiosity. "How does he know?" I asked my mother. The fibers in me were twisting and vibrating. I became filled with the possibility of his life continuing and decided to speak to him directly, hoping to convince him that his death need not be imminent.

I go to my father and I say "Why do you think you are going to die?" His feeling is more one of resignation or tiredness, than any specific illness. I ask him matter-of-factly to take off his clothes so that I may look at his body. He does so and his body appears to be fine, a bit shorter and stockier than I remember, but ruddy and glowing. I see immediately that he is perfectly well and able to live for a very long time. I tell him with conviction that there's no reason for him to continue on this course, being wholly alive with many things yet to do. As I tell him this, we are walking through a woods, now up a slight incline to a clearing. My father seems joyous to hear the news. He accepts it with a kind of privacy that he's always had, savoring it for himself, indicating that he hopes I won't make a public thing of it. There is a kind of charged excitement between us.

In 1965, my father was hit by a car and pronounced dead. I asked for his first set of architect's drawing tools, wrapped in a chamois case he'd sewn himself, each metal pencil and compass enclosed in its own soft pocket, each a potential source of precision and invention, given a hand to hold it.

[1/13/76]

La Revolution

For A. K. B.

Everything is so agreeable, tangential, so light
of foot.
         Tangerine, all pungent with its leaves intact.

Still, revolution is your quietest intent,
it throbs through your kindness like a double bass
without amplification,

but you are persistent and grow a callous of light
from so often stroking the gut strings.
                                You hold

its body next to yours, in the air,
and when you play in the key of C
molecules forget their lesser purpose
                                and turn swiftly
              breathing the new physics.

              I listen. You invite me to care on a grand scale.
              What must I leave behind me?

Like you, I give the finger to
standing still. I'm tactile.
Here are all my fingers to place inside yours.

Looked at, loosely, within any frame of reference,
I could seem predictable.
Don't be fooled. Bumpy ovals of color thrill me.
Tangentially.

              I count on your intelligence, with or without you
sitting there. Still, I want more.

Perfection begins to hurt because
love feels dangerous
                    and only one of us is you,
only one of us is taking the other's temperature.
But that could be over-simplified, since you often choose
not to tell.

What do you notice, awake? I notice I'm afraid to break in on
the fluidity. My dreams ask questions,
                              the ones' I've thought about
                              but can't speak.
Sleeping next to you, your shadow
wrestles with mine. The glow is Kirlian. What you hide
in the revolution pours intimately through the dark.
It's effect can't be measured in the "real" world.

All controls break down. The sheets convey your deepest sigh
to my body. You are not alarmed because we don't say a word.

                                                [2/21/76]

Coincidental

Half of my friends accuse me of excess
(waiting on line and trusting in inches)
The other half lean
and have given up glossy fenders with their little pockmarks of rust

It is comforting to know that these same accusations
keep company among the ducks fighting for bread from your fingers
using their beaks with concentrated fury

Revulsion has been mainly a failure
and so has dabbling,
                  while exactness can rest
in one hand, smoothly
as a fertilized egg
                Without knowing, one might be listening
for the crack which would merely indicate a vulnerability,
the delicate parabolic strength in the egg's curve
beyond our power to reduce it

Physics becomes more cheerful each day and delights
in breaking the laws of nature

While quantums flow backwards, our children on skate boards
are pulled up into the sky
in the same way that Christ was swallowed by white clouds

One might call this a sort of rapprochement—the unthinkable light

You must elaborate or ascend   One chooses to pay attention

to the movement, an output of plant roots or
the possible expansion under each arm
where the breath might flow freely   and in dignity

We feel how all the little clutches of the body seem finalized
as though some law of physics told us to hold ourselves tightly
and not let any part fall out
                   any messy tear
Rigorous methods have been established to capture the elusive,
a fanatic devotion to statistics and controls
                       but

we secretly pray to ghosts as they hover among the teeth of gears
We feel our muscle systems quivering, as though trying to get loose

A great urge to be down-to-earth seems to show up in each generation
You can slice it as you would a flatworm for a microscopic study
or shuffle it or randomly select
well-bathed individuals and place them in an antiseptic
atmosphere
and still the tiny jiggles of light persist,
as though some precedent of joy insisted on having its way—
a full tank, a sunny day, a mailbox stuffed with envelopes

One of the Chapters

How could you be by halves,
behooved and beholden?

Held   but, oh, I wanted to be held

and wanted to fall
through the net's tiny squares like sunlight through cheesecloth.

What was expected of me
                    and did I want my urge?
And certainly I recognized marriage and children.

I recognized coils and nets
and didn't think you could be double in Iowa.

But by then and for keeps I was keeping.
Seeping into the necessity
of contradiction.

But let's stop
to fill in the special quality of isolation—
a men's university town,
women cutting parsley and watching the green.

I still remember how it seemed a life.
                    I came away laughing.
Somehow I absorbed the air itself, out of the air,
because I don't remember anyone
telling me,
          so that women have trouble with poetry
except for Emily.

Do you think I can have suffered? Do relationships keep?
I had to buy health. I gave up other options. But it was temporary.

This loose voice, no less, is crucial.
Other places pinch, but not really
to act on music suffered in the brain.

Everyone's childhood is several years later and less physical,
while the lover who promises parts of his body   lies in his body
sharing his cravings, wanting to, and can't

except in each construction
with somebody. Some body.

Questioning the tools. Looking at Picasso with you.
But isn't autobiography on the alert for bread?
It must be sniffing.

We realize how much we need, exactly, and personally,
as in a London bookstall, wondering if I could afford to buy,
with the heart of Sara Crewe in my heart, the same heart
and her penny for a hot bun
as her velvet dress becomes smaller and smaller and her father
forgets her.

Note: This poem includes and responds to phrases from Jane Cooper's essay, "Nothing has
been used in the manufacture of this poetry that could have been used in the manufacture
of bread" (*Maps & Windows*, Macmillan, 1974).

Flowers

Changing water. Adding aspirin. Nitrogen, potash or
sugar (white) to keep limpness from descending
upon these purple and magenta asters with broad golden centers
and petals packed in two rows making fringe above
green spread leaves, still alive. Keep cutting stems
to retain the vertical pull of water up into
the barely charged life.

.

She said there was a tiny charge of energy *still*, like a cord moving between
me and the child—a girl—though its body life had stopped after four
months, only one leg intact on the fetus. "It's better," the doctor said
"Nature knows best," he said, at the end.

That was ten years ago. He was pulling me along on an immaculate silver
table, larger than a serving tray, I thought, sheet over me then, white linen,
and their faces soothing, shapes of words and eyes I couldn't identify.
Something inside me had broken, though I tried to hold it in.

.

In the white stone pitcher I always place flowers.
First water, then the spiked metal frog
where each flower is stuck in arrangements of
height, darkness or intensity of bloom. The accidents
interest me. The Japanese effect of less.
Space showing its wandering shape between leaves
and the sudden curve of a stem
dying slowly towards what light is
in the room. One forgets about hunger,
absorbed in the fuchsia and the mauve.

Dear Laura, In December

Dear Laura, in the pause that has lengthened
      between us   I imagine your face
          as David described it—Mexican
   with Chinese eyes—
          sniffing face powder from Hong Kong
            so white where it fell
on the rug   among blue flowers   Christmas
    morning   There is always someone
        about to be born   The snow
          falls lightly first
  and peregrine falcon waits
         on a high branch
    Even your boredom has the fragrance
         of alertness
in this white tissue   green smalltown air

Our mother (yours or mine) is the only one
     given us   so
       it is hard to allow
         ragged weather
under her striped wing and talon
      In the Rauschenberg work you sent, she is
        standing on toes   head tipped back
  as though hunting for something airborne
              not there yet
      Inky blue fades into femur,
breasts ballooning like swimsuit ads
and her own very round thighs
        kissing each other's
            tallow and wicklight

What is that darkness? she murmurs
    inside herself   pushing it
     tentatively
       out   What hope
  she wraps you in lightly
        as Chinese face powder
She sees you are a rose with its petals folded
    as if in summer   sleeping authentically
    Or she sees behind you
  a shadow   somebody's   out the window
       falling

I want to remember this season in layers
                    of color   the year I was ten
        and discovered pointillism
                            red blue green gold silver
        spreading slow hot points
                        on the tree
                    because my mother started up in us this urge
            for more

It was cold in San Francisco on the 24th (before
                the clean rains and the five moaning earthquakes)
            I made chili and the phone began
                    ringing   Christmas eve on the street
                        and everyone wanting a bite
            Frances on the way to a party
                            dressed up in orange and pink satins
                opening their little lights like poppies
        Mark in gangster pinstripes recited Wallace Stevens
            I love them for how they imagine their lives
                    into being   You were
            sitting with your "vibrant and colorful" mom
                    in the kitchen in Kutztown, Pa.   sipping tea
        whispering inside yourself a constant storm of
                who and who or who and me
                        waiting for some red pillow life
            to discover you   refusing anybody's claim but wanting
                a stranger to pull you into
                        car lights   dark streets   snow

I went out to find wood   I could feel how dark it was
                and wanted to make a fire for us   My lover had come
                        a great distance   bringing violets
        and a Japanese comforter   silky with falcons,
                beige-feathered and gliding above a blue sea
                    He wanted to comfort me
                        When he's here, I believe
                it's enough
                                        David keeps trying
                    to feel the insides of things   to open
        the morning's wrappings before it's time
                Tomorrow he's ten   he can't keep his hands off

Locations

For Bill Evans, jazz pianist

Light forgetting itself   light falling loosely
deep into May

Trying to listen to all that presses up
from under each side
of the seam

Holes where something gives in
to a pulse   careful stitches unraveling

cross-hatch of insulated wires
black slow curves among the poles
street slopes   here
in shadow where houses
lean on each other

but light still
catching white oil tank   distinct against
blue haze above bay water

Pollution soothes us in early evening
we breathe in and forget
coffee no longer hot   wind coming up
flapping the shades

Red metal pot the color of poppies

His love
the spot on the white tablecloth
after dinner

•

To give up
finally   to stop holding
the infant idea   how deep
you've been told to hurt,

to dissemble the structure
of wounds which choose
to resemble one another

Someday, because he was an exquisite set
of gestures, you thought
you would escape
the yearning to be surprised infinitely

A home inside yourself

Your body held unto itself

There were ways of talking

.

He plays his piano in big cities
and now you are alone with him
in the full amplification
of ambiguous chords which he trusts
silence to justify

What is waiting for you
to fall into
big saxophone body
pulling from another side
of the seam
of music no longer
automatically
dropping

An effort to leave the window
justifies the question of
which is more important:

to witness
last light of mauve sponge sky

or, an inclination towards sound
drifting through the cities
where you listen
to what he isn't telling you,
clearly ambiguous
and totally intimate

.

How she notices is a formal fact
clearly evident as a chip of paint
knocked off perfect white flow

where someone's brush tried to see a wall

Amplification attempts to make it all
all right
and in times of sorrow
a voice turned up loud
can be a true resonance

Still, some sound was too pretty

an easy beat
where you could get stuck,
not finding out

Two trout bought for supper, to please his mouth,
now softening under their scales
She'd know if their eyes were dead
Lights just went out
The scales were silver and excited her
in a room she didn't talk about

.

Summer, such a little place

full of fish in rivers leaping   The apples out,
red with yellow streaking their sides,
not so glamorous as stores promised
but pulling low on branches next to the road

All in heaviness
to be crushed into softness   Her sweet throat
Cider drinks   gravel you hear first
from the driveway
before the shadow appears   and then
the visual body of the guest

.

These acts of attention   to fill in
all the gaps
where his body keeps going away

Now That the Subjunctive is Dying

for A.

The interior pulse of loosely closed mouth after love,
    roof and tongue in that pause of
        not what might be, but learning
  each seam of you, how plum and
           undulant life of testicles goes on
           tenderly, soles of feet
    in water, yours, if only candlelight
          piles up on porcelain edge
             of tub to fall off with glide
               of soapy skin.

Now clouds blowing towards us, the dark's away
    in a mid-day light that might have been Italian,
       pigeons, on the other side of glass five floors up
          in wind marked with faint dust streaks,
    swoop down, curve in arcs, cut sideways
        given depth by milk-colored stucco
         buildings, shadows in the old style,
    summery, and fire ladders climbing down or
        up to antennae. We are lavish
        rooms with many doorways that open out.
         Your face, if that is your body standing there,
  suggests the hand on a doorknob that could be
        possibly
           turning.

•

When I left you, those hours, and went for my Saturday massage, Mary,
laying her small brown Sicilian hands on my body, felt the tightness move
off. "Did you feel it go?" she said. "It left. You are so open today. Something
is happening. The door may shut. But he's opened it. He's standing in it.
Listening. To what you might be able to say. What he can hear."

•

touch to tell you   listen, to touch everything

this is   this day, in which someone didn't run away

•

Sleep after little sleep, sweet afternoon as if
not disfigured by anyone's time, only bits of fog

hide in air. I lie on your bed reading Rilke and
copying his best lines into my notebook, wake up hours

later, deep in snow drifts, pen still in hand, as though writing.

We were all night finding each others' tongues and knees,
we were all that could have been, in our own finishing.

Still, sleep has taken me into late afternoon with
the corner of your bedspread pulled up over me while

you, on your back, in air, above the couch in the other room,
discover your body below and a girl dreaming of a door.

from *Each Next* narratives [1980]

this. notes.

new year.

Dear other, I address you in sentences. I need your nods and I hear your echoes. There is a forward movement still, as each word is a precedent for what new order. You can hear a distant habit. The sound of a low gas flame discharging. Even a hiss is only soothing because it is dark and nearing the shorter perimeters. When I run into boredom, I shift into another's past.

(She was "in a fury" and she wept in spite of herself. His letter told the usual stores in all the old ways. She swallowed them whole. Then came the nausea. She wanted a "flow" she thought, but in the translation it was corrected, displacing the *o* and substituting *a*. She could give herself to an accident. She was looking out the window.)

This is the Year of Our Lord. Every year we always have these difficulties. The sound of water splatting from the bathroom, heard through the kitchen, the clank of a soap dish. "I'm going to take a shower," David bragged, striding through the room on his twelfth birthday.

I tried to protect myself especially well. I had time to play at domesticity this year. Three-quarters cup of bourbon in the chocolate-covered bourbon balls. There were many occasions and I was there in a different skirt. I went to the sales with her. She believed in that and built up her vocabulary like a wardrobe purchased during ten different years, but only on December 26th.

One man said of another that he was committed to the sentence. I sentence you. I could hear the terseness of his sentences and how seductive it seemed to move the words always towards a drop in the voice. What did it mean to be flat? Was there a principle of denial? Of manipulation? I'm worried. He is embarrassed.

The French workers often raised their voices on the Blvd. des Minimes and along the tiny alleys of the Ile St. Louis. You could hear questions rising to the windows of the sixth floor of the Hôtel St. Louis, although the bathroom, if you wanted to take a tub bath, was on the fourth floor. Voices raised at the ends of sentences, as though all were in question.

It made you want to look out the window. You could sniff the momentous occasion. The bakery opening its door each morning to a view of *pain au chocolat* on trays. *Entrez, s'il vous plaît.*

I wanted, suddenly, to speak French because of certain French women thinking about layers, thinking *in* layers, but as yet not translated. They had moved ahead but not in a line. It occurred to me that growing up inside of, yet opposing, a tradition peculiarly French and masculine appeared to give them a certain authority because the tradition itself assumed a dialectical plane and invited the next position, while echoing "I baptize thee in the name of the father and the son."

(She questioned the wistful half-truths he gained solace from, using a certain Rapidograph pen with its fine black lines. He gave the boy a drawing pen. He said it was for art. The boy's face broke open and filled with light. Enlightened. Boyish and tender.)

I question these wistful half-truths and why I sink into silence around them. Now that I've made the decision to attempt a separation from their hold on me, I am released into sentences. The gas heater is a constant I could compare.

I change my mind every day. I think of my mother's love. The antique bracelet she gave me with dozens of flowers etched into the tarnished brass. A line from Kunitz surfaces from the year I was twenty-one. "A single color oversweeps the field." That is all my memory provides of it. But to understand truly, you'd need the lines before it, building up to that crescendo that thrilled me. A vast field of scarlet poppies in the south of France . . . a movement in front of one. As a season. In a second. The forward movement of slow motion. Even then, the field. Of many flowers moving at their own speeds. Not one then two then three. But moving. Split. Second. Rushing into petals.

That was a peculiar passion I do not often encounter in the poetry of the late '70s, but do not want to deny. That urgency we call romantic, but which might actually be, in part, the willingness to be told lies. That rush. How I've wanted it. His romance.

(He tried to deflect her anger. He tried to mystify her by leaving half of everything out. He made her laugh. He knew what she wanted. In her "worst moments" she wanted obsession, obliteration of choice.)

You are against confession, because it's embarrassing. I want to embarrass you. To feel your confusion. Someone's rhythm sneaking in again. Sharing a language. The osmosis of rubbing up. Communing.

I'll never make candy again. It is a relief to write this music. Who does it belong to? "*Who can I turn to?*" Las Vegas crooners with their soft, slimy hair styles. Feel the lyric hit, anyway. As soft as sniffing it. Where's the kleenex?

Christmas is over and "I'm glad," I said to David. "It's such a pressure building up." He smiled, being twelve now, and not satisfied, even though we tried to cover all the branches with icicles and double strands of lights. Next year, it's snowing.

Lily, Lois & Flaubert: the site of loss

for Robert Glück

"How is she?" I asked.

"She's well. She is just fine," he said. "My Lily is back. I have my family back. I can take the sitter home now. Would you like me to do that? The tires are bad, so I go up hills slowly. But Lily doesn't mind."

Who is Lily? I think. I try to remember which one Lily is. Lily must be one third of his nuclear family. The other third is his Aunt Cora, sitting in an airplane above Los Angeles, thin trail of white smoke drifting always above and behind him. One can almost hear the gossamer command of her voice in his childhood, filtered like light falling perpetually upon him. Her shadow is a light jacket, his little coat from the third grade.

Listening to him speak of Lily, I decided that he must be speaking of his lover. I thought I understood him. That is, I immediately provided a set of images from which to identify this object of his affection. To my ear, his all-embracing acceptance of Lily sounded romantic and excessive. I felt a bit jealous. I compared his feeling for her to a cloud of dust escaping from a vacuum cleaner. But as the dust cleared, things took on their true shapes and I understood that Lily was his dog. "White Lily of my family," he called her. "I wanted a family," I once heard him say to himself.

His voice was a kind of scenery behind the scrim one sees at the front of the stage, at the apron of the stage where Lily was forever wagging her tail. Lily, who had been lost, was now back in his arms. There existed among us a scenario, stitching together our lives at intervals: this tin can of dogfood he opened and spooned into a dish for her linked Lily's love of dogfood to his love of Lily to my romantic projection of his "other life."

.

Phillipe S. has a dog called Lois. From the beginning of our friendship, this fact has been clearly established. Phillipe feeds Lois *blanquette de veau* to gain her trust. He likes to think of Lois as something sacred, a sacrament as only the French use the word. He likes to lick his chops when he thinks of the pure prosody of life with Lois, the sheer grammar of Lois when she gushes her dog speech—often a series of sharp barks, as though a ribbon of sound were emitted spontaneously.

Phillipe often imagines Lois ordering a five course meal with all the correct wines. Her commanding use of the vernacular provides him with clear directives, a perpetual reassurance of order in his otherwise muddled life.

Lois gives him vigorous argument as well as propriety. And her wag assures him, even in those hours alone, when he feels the subject falling away from the predicate and that odd chill rise up to drench his solar plexus, when the sentence, as he's known it, begins to dismantle itself.

.

We have a dog at our house. His name is Rover. He's hardly ever around. Sometimes we call him Flaubert, to introduce a second possibility—as, for instance, on a grayish day when you pull up the shade on waking, with the hope of orange emerging somewhere among the cloud layers—just a small gash, even, as when my friend's old work pants developed a rip and you could see his muscular thigh showing through, a bit of tawny skin, though the trousers were loose and not normally the kind of garment you'd attribute to sexual arousal.

Flaubert, as a nickname, provides an immediate source of imagery. A guest walking in and hearing you call out "Flaubert . . . Flaubert???" might enter a different context than he thought his steps were leading to—a configuration of narrow lanes and dark doorways opening onto courtyards, or an acknowledgement of certain social issues he had hoped to dismiss as buried.

The wine you serve at dinner takes on an entirely different bouquet, a brickier color, haunted by an aftertaste of vineyards in the Dordogne. It hardly matters that Flaubert does not come in, wagging his tail and performing the set of trick his former master taught him. His name is enough.

"Flaubert . . . Flaubert?" Now the guest begins to ease toward that seam where the stretch of his former life is stitched to this room, where Flaubert's remembered barks form a discourse that still perforates the common silence.

The decision

Today a package at my door. Brown wrapping paper, imprinted three times with the same foreign currency—a golden cow with herringbone wings and tail, the number 20 under its belly and the word EIRE stamped in white against a marine blue background.

·

I was looking through my collection of black silk beauty marks. *Mouches pour bal* cut from a black field of silk at *42, Rue de Chabrol*. A horse. Two horses pulling a carriage. Star. Heart. Star, heart, half-moon. A gentleman in a top hat. Dashing off, as they say. I was looking for a mark. A sign to place abruptly there, on the white field of the paper. To hold your attention for an instant only. Then to set free the threads which would loosen themselves from the interior. You thought you were somewhere else. This would move the prediction you had made for yourself. Now you would be riding, either on the bare back of the horse or inside the carriage where you wouldn't be seen but could look out from the gold leaf casements. As you like.

·

She had been occupied. As in "occupied zone." She had gone to see the Peruvian gold exhibit at the Hall of Science. She decided to wear her gold, imagining how to dress for the event. Gold circles through her ears. The twisted gold strands, always now on the middle finger of the right hand; she did not want to encourage misinterpretation. Also the gold chain, given her by a lover who had handed it to her in a tiny scarlet bag drawn shut with silk threads. But the chain was not around her neck when she felt for it. Nothing would stay in place in her memory, looking for the chain as through pages in a magazine. What she could remember of the last two days and on what occasions she took it off, the only occasions being swimming and making love. She pulled the blanket halfway off the bed and found nothing.

·

After looking at the Peruvian gold, they were filled with the idea of simplicity. They tried to remember who it was that sacrificed so many live victims from their own source, the Aztecs or the Incas? That night, while he undressed, instead of watching his body she hunted again for the gold chain. She found it at the very end of the bed where the sheet tucked in.

She placed it on the white dresser without comment. Then she made love to him.

·

I wanted to send you one of the three stamps from Ireland because of the field of marine blue which might suggest water and how deep it has been known to travel below the surface. There was a lake, for instance, at the bottom of some caves near Alt Aussee, where an enormous European art treasure had been hidden by members of Hitler's S.S. troops. Secured boxes of treasure had been dropped into the lake. Gold and jewels. They thought to drain the bottom of the lake at the end of the war and recover the treasure. Divers were sent down and did not come back. Four died. Separately. There seemed to be no bottom to the lake. And yet they know the treasure is still there. There are several who cannot let go of this thought.

·

She feels somewhat safe in the water. She knows he doesn't care for it much. She needs to know how deep it is. She looks for the markers at the side of the pool, although she has swum in lakes and has felt their muddy bottoms on the soles of her feet. It is an alarming experience and thus difficult to give in to the sensuality of this physical surprise. But on that day, she wanted to turn her back on her fear. They took off their clothes at the edge of the water. She put the gold chain in a little heap on top of her folded blouse, where she could see it. His wife was watching them but she didn't want to come in. They had never seen each other's bodies. Something passed between them in the water. They looked beyond each other, as if there were no mystery. She swam to the other side. It was a warm, late afternoon and the moon was already out, very white and pared down. A flicker, or was it a mockingbird, lit in the topmost branches of the only tree at the lake's edge. It was then she began to imagine she understood the gestures of birds. She watched them closely during the following year and was able to make several startling decisions with split-second timing.

Lena Pergola

When he uses
the word it
clatters, it returns
loud where the
word is a
marble. The
word will never
come back but
any word. It
does use. Back
does come back.

.

When I'm lying in my crib, was I
was hands wrapped around inside white.
Mittens cotton. Not to get out.

Waiting we feel but not
when the Chicago "El" goes by
against the window. Crib tied
on outside track. Light tied to inch.
Infinite exactly inch, feeling bars of it separate.

.

He kept saying
suddenly it wasn't
a river when
it was ice.
His voice was
never there all
the time the
light was yellow
the crib bars
were white. The
"El" went up.
We were in
my buggy. Everything
was in air
and the same
size. Little particles

of black but
in the white.

·

She jumped out from the dark.
Her name is Lena Pergola in the hallway.
She liked to eat spaghetti. There were big spoons.
And all the spaghetti for everyone falling off itself
on the platter. With red tomato sauce.
She hitchhiked with someone handsome like my uncle who shaved.
I stood in his bathroom first. I was almost up. Steam all over
the air and sweet bottles. "You like me, hunh?"

·

Thinking someone was
Jesus again and
daddy had chances.
Keep saying suddenly.
Who out from
the dark hallway?
Very long with
light some to
see the something
behind it the
dark "boo" or
"mooooo," who you
is to be
nice and told
me about first
and things I
didn't dark not
go not a
moment if down
the stairs and
down the elevator
up the door
where light is
out after they
tied you not
to suck thumb.
I was white.
I was inside
a closed bite.

Of God any
small any will
have wings or
a he or
under the bed
with crown and
sceptre both king
and queen in
dust cloud and
black or mouse
not stared at
anything don't look
it is under
the corner, or . . .

.

Keep saying suddenly why the tidy way in the white sink
day. The silver razor pulled down his cheek. Black trousers,
white undershirt. Things go happen. Ago long hallway on the road.
And music inside his horn. Lena, Lena, Lena Pergola.

"His words stink," she said.
My hands tied.
"Take the El."
Go up.

Somebody who is hooked on the color red

is just coming into your blue room
which ruins another person's life.

You can get right off the hook.

To put out his own scare you have a child. Enough of these goings.

You'll proliferate now, thoughts misbegotten to strike through
every face truly. People whom you are.

Getting on with this blank, are you saying
one should follow when the position comes?

I think that door is closed.

If only he didn't close. You shouldn't waste metric time.
The mental passage is somewhat over. That will occur to you
strongly. Nobody's knocking.

How do you say "Bring in folks," "One guy," "Breakthrough."
We all go up and everybody
gets his limit and his hope. Your empty page needs
voices and very little to do, where you stand off-base, forming various
whites from the window.

(Females who have never lived a female life, when in fact they need
two.)

What you'll refer to. A dream of separate rooms.
The red room. The blue room.

You're in the present. That little place opens when you drop inside.

Your fresh start.

Notes re: Echo

for Steve Benson

September 4

The sunset again, a favorite time of the horizon he might wish to play out.

Less than what was meant, as a last point of resistance, then its answer or echo or next.

It could be in the identification of spectrum order. A color which didn't include red. Or, if one had the temperament, all the possible red categories.

Values of red.

.

Coffee takes its immediate effect; a system had been registering its blurrrr. Things were not right. "Not quite," he said.

The holidays and their deliberate, agonizingly habitual tables. Too much animal fat. Beef ribs and lamb ribs in succession, in sauces with equally talented cooks. Focus on the gesture and an appropriate "ummmm good" dissevers him from a clear path that had achieved a balance he now took for granted in the wake of hiccups.

September 5

That pressure behind you pushing with increasing lightness, the beginning of September, the fourth, at noon, exactly, and all the news falling out of your little cubbyhole, smelling of cheap purple ink. Interpretations now. Messages from me to you. A room of faces looking for the good, the true and the beautiful.

Plan 1: Wearing a slit skirt will divert their expectations.
Plan 2: The decision not to eat an apple in front of them.
Intimacy retrieved. Laying down the law. Putting a boundary between us:

All of you are (A). I, alone, am (B). But we share this perception and, in that, we all are (C), together, filled with anticipation of the future.
Plan 3: Here is my syllabus.

September 6

Elements of disorder. A sweet disorder in the dress. The idea of order in Key West. Disorder and Early Sorrow. Order me a beer.
September 7

Dear Narcissus,

Is language, in fact, the pool? Looking into your words as if they represented a surface of water (Narcissus gazes with longing, trying to find himself), do I then find me, a word I know? Yes. No. Some deflection, in-flexing of where we might overlap. Sitting on your lap, a word comes back at me, as an echo. So I divest myself of the disembodied me . . . Echo is She, who watches Narcissus look for himself and returns him to himself, slightly altered, by her very attentiveness.

Where am I?

Love,

Echo

September 8

The echo is blunt-eared. Narcissus blundered.
"You are really gone."   "This is really school."

·

"What makes you most anxious about this class?"

One woman wrote, "I am afraid that what I want to say will not be important enough."

On reading this statement, another woman remarked: "You could drop that part. We're really beyond that."

September 9

What you admire unequivocally and love wholeheartedly is not mine.

September 10

Dear Narcissus,

While you were gone, I divided into two even more distinct territories.

·

Walking up to a new edge, I discovered in myself an old mute. But I stayed, allowing my curiosity to teethe on the silence. A hope for mutation? A belief in mutability. It was, of course, a question of language. Of a code shared by the interior of four fingers and a thumb who knew each other's openings and closings. Knew how to make a fist, the form of which I recognized and hated, while feeling an odd affection and curiosity for each of the parts.

In what appeared to be home, I was also alone. I missed our talks, which always pull me somewhere new, but in your friendly red wagon with its creaky wheels. So I began to write about my grandfather, who was out-of-order, displaced from his known function and terrain. These stories were written within a solid and digested tradition of linked sentences. Achieving their life gave me a kind of satisfaction I'd not known.

Why, then, do I trust your language enough to enter it? I trust it because it is both watchful and fluid, allowing the variants of yourself to have voice. Am I who you hear?

Love,
Echo

September 11

His words. How they tone up, then polarize or identify certain pleasures. Activate some as yet unexercised part. But the beautiful surface is always involved with seduction. And what of the darker, colder water? One cannot deny its pull.

How, then, to hold on to the *who* you think you are. The image in water shifts, according to the light's impact, and currents we cannot wholly predict.

It's always were.

And we are sifting. We are the foggy morning's grey shape moving . . . and beyond the bridge, nothing but clear blue skies.

·

"Echo watches over her shoulder on another rock on the other side of the stream, resigned, as Narcissus is constantly on the way, surprised."

from *Something (even human voices)*
in the foreground, a lake [1984]

Something (even human voices) in the foreground, a lake

A definite mountain (the upper with tableaux), foul water.

The air was back of the house, my knee sweet, intervening roses and heavy-hanging apricot boughs as the morning advanced, an imposition of isolated will upon the deck chairs, the docks and fragments (even human voices), the watery glitter of bits of food afloat on the water's surface. That hole, the size of fifty cents in someone's childhood. You always called "Here, little fishy" when you dropped the orange and green flakes into the round opening. I often looked for a dead one. Even a light bulb fooled me. "You are glad it wasn't what you thought it was," you told me. You were accurate but on another morning, I noticed, while sitting in a chair, listening to you speak a halting Italian on the borrowed telephone, a small silver fish with clouded eye lying back-to-back with its reflection. Anything is interchangeable with a small net. You know that.

They did not make conversation.

A lake as big, the early evening wind at the bather's neck. Something pulling (or was it rising up) green from the bottom. You could lie flat and let go of the white creases. You could indulge your fear of drowning in the arms of shallow wet miles. You did not open your mouth, yet water poured into openings, making you part. Bone in the throat. That dark blue fading, thinning at the edges. On deck chairs with bits of flowered cloth across their genitals, the guests called out in three languages and sometimes pointed, commenting on the simple beauty of bought connection. The swan-like whiteness of the day. That neck of waves. There was always a tray with small red bottles. And pin-pointed attentions, at each slung ease.

Anna, in lawn chair endeavor.

Anna extended, brilliant legalities cast in her secret place in the mountains with another's white satin gown against the bluest shadows. Their uniform extended limbs and tiny leaves impressed by a suggestion. Raking that space between us, our teeth, Anna, and your glittery rings showing all you don't have, oh the collar folded. Body's little mistakes won't look at you now. In the corners, never in sneakers, you prowl the page of a large heavy man and wish to be a signature he could touch and remember later and pay for.

Becoming famous and powerful.

To each other, she is as if the sun were oddly powerful, borne in her palinquin mind, her grammar moving in the lag (into) a narrower cut, slammed on a map of fixed color, crimson perhaps, like a tear in the surface of isolation, her brain the extenuated appreciation, the cold space it leaves as it blows by. Oh happy speed, marshes here, mahogany blue boats for one foot (startled by that flatter water's intimacy), clenched in the same style he remembers. Beautiful hair to take care of. The selfish ruined shine of her.

The sun opens and begins to work.

Not quite rubbed smooth, increased in size, they talk often of the old marriages. A boy with black hair is younger when he looks in the window, into what is darkness later, at her legs, in which she concentrates all of literature, re-arranging how and what to yell at him. His face shifts and reloads the rectangle holding the frame's air. Where he was, voices shouting from the opposite window. You know them.

Anna ("Are you looking at me?"), if not.

A lack of confidence stiffening this patch of hand over the body's bronzing. Abbronzato, working at it, and "Do you like it?" Her leg aside his arm. Arm against friends'. Galactic and childish in white while pulling at hem. Blinking little nipples before the keyhole drift where he lifts a path of white to display what is his little worry. All your hoarded blemishes could be big ones gathering a life (subcutaneous) against you. The man in red bikini buys you houses. You show your present, then he takes it away under that smile and a change of clothes. Turquoise bikini, rolling over from the day confirmed as yesterday. Neither headlines, nor even finer print. Looking for "ponentino" (little Western wind, to us), lifting your dress for them. She drifts in from bath in Hollywood white satin and already you are craving it, but you can buy anything and think it doesn't work. Working-out once, the glaze pulled back its gauzy robe. But you would not give what was yours much.

Covertly, her husband('s eyes).

The boy with white apron hurriedly, tray in hand, the usual small coffees and head not visible due to position of green shutters,

his red comb,

Later and tense, looking too big for the body.

Something has leaked out. I could have gone away. Dropping precipitously into the other life, uniformly spaced drinks and a heavy leaf supporting this September air. Oh receive us, house and terraces. Open nine light-bulbs and let the doors have crossed locks. This second language accommodates more bathing. You offer cheese, which you have divided to keep us hungry for a later precise event.

She had a woman friend.

Part of the collar folded under.

Careless of all his advice, flowers.

With the ability of some, the flowers, the sight of him bending the night's two lakes, that untrained relation of craving to thought. She dreams of him as a woman whose dark hair has been recently bleached. A sympathetic Harlow blonde. White satin without seams. She seems to row in one lake and sail on the other. At night, the splash does not travel far. The others stay up endlessly—eating and drinking (things unutterably sweet).

They travel, heading for "Three Columns,"
the late demolished.

Wishing for credentials bearing the high arch of the narrow foot, and crav-
ing those little knitted caps the foreign flautist always wore at his perfor-
mances, they decide as a group. He brings his powders and the colored
map, she the blue feather which has long signified a private distance.
"Africa in August assures spring beaches," that's why, and the "food we all
love," considered in detail. Hunting by camera. Perfect clicks behind glass.
They vote in the pouches of twilight, are of one mind. Trays arrive, their
leader waves his flag-colored moccasins and cannot contain the certain ex-
citement of perfect greed. "Already," he explains, "we are on the alert for
fatal attractions and particularly noteworthy frescoes. Wives, you know
your portion."

Small pyramid, marginal attention.

In the left hand margin of her ivory gown, purchased at great expense and
with a certain spontaneity, the flea from someone else's couch, perceptibly
there in its brief jumps. This was her vacation, and the source of future re-
countings. They learn the latest dance, how to shoot with bows and ar-
rows. Take pictures of themselves doing these things.

"The certainty of Byzantine tendencies," she reads.

This sweet curl and cold cove of Acanthus, oh leaf-bearing thought in stone, when we consider what has stood! (Strokes the feather in her pocket.) Gift of thumb, its opposites; time inside a person, worn threads of your cape dazzle us, oh lover of birds we didn't notice! Our muscles ache from the simple climb. These stones the length of tubs, with their tiny ridges, catch us. Behind shutters the dark. Eyes of she who cuts and washes. Cuts and washes.

Madonna hypothesis.

Down the middle keeps tearing. Is torn and wants to.

In the "Eugubian Tablets," we turn.

I am the leader. Here is your tablet. Where is the table? Bring me red wine. This is your alphabet, to be written backwards. Untie the boat. Your hands will be woolen. Cover your ears. We move into stone. Perugia is our rival.

.

I am the leader. Here is your tablet. Where is the table? Bring me red wine. This is your alphabet, to be written backwards. Untie the boat. Your hands will be woolen. Cover your ears. We move into stone. Perugia is our rival.

Stunned, magnificent, cylindrical.

With only me and you, racks of lamb in the spring of the dark, rough wood, The Octagon, two kinds of red not easily compatible, the thinnest intent of denial. Meanwhile,

those tiny strawberries piled in crystal, *fraises des bois*. Your sapling shining. Balustrade of the long wish. Someone smaller standing in shadow, as though moving, but not here. Holding my hand.

In white, she who bathed.

Everywhere, rooms are leading to other rooms. The brain, she thinks is her corridor and her strict casement when she is a window. It is believed that she understands partially, but cannot speak, except haltingly, and about nothing in particular.

Medusa's hair was snakes. Was thought, split inward.

for Frances Jaffer

I do not wish to report on Medusa directly, this variation of her
writhing. After she gave that voice a shape, it was the trajectory itself
in which she found her words floundering and pulling apart.

Sometimes we want to talk to someone who can't hear us.
Sometimes we're too far away. So is a shadow
a real shadow.

When he said "red cloud," she imagined *red*
but he thought *cloud* (this dissonance in which she was feeling
trapped, out-of-step, getting from here to there).

Historical continuity
accounts for knowing what dead words point to,

a face staring down through green leaves as the man looks up
from tearing and tearing again at his backyard weeds. His red dog sniffs
at what he's turned over. You know what I mean.
We newer people have children who learn to listen as *we* listen.

M. wanted her own.
Kept saying *red dog. Cloud.*
Someone pointing to it while saying it. Someone discovering stone.

Medusa trying to point with her hair.
That thought turned to venom.
That muscle turning to thought turning
to writhing out.

We try to locate blame, going backwards.
I point with my dog's stiff neck
and will not sit down,
the way that girl points her saxophone at the guitar player
to shed light
upon his next invention. He attends her silences, between keys,
and underscores them with slow referents.

Can she substitute *dog* for *cloud*, if *red* comes first?
Red tomato.
Red strawberry.

As if all this happens on the ocean one afternoon in July,
red sunset soaking into white canvas. The natural world.
Darkness does eventually come down.
He closes her eye in the palm of his hand.
The sword comes down. .

Now her face rides above his sails, her hair her splitting tongues.

Flashes of light or semaphore waves, the sound
of rules, a regularity from which the clouds drift
into their wet embankments.

from *Notes preceding trust* [1987]

boundayr

The seizing of the blue social level, the red duality inert the yellow body forming intimate contact, essential string, the beige of hemp and wall, green responding, green sado/shadow bottle, the plum enables us, the black beyond our hours will satisfy this encounter,

substantial white of chair the presence in the world of non-primary blue. Red enables us to be distinct *and* substantial, at some point we must inhabit ourselves, the evidence is mauve and lively with grey borders, to know, to feel, even *be* the inheriting white, the celery, that light with which we regulate, become pink and peach, we blush and are fruit, we bruise but did blossom formally, we are halfway there, we are capable of giving the ultra aquamarine, we are absence of carnelian. Now

you are in the violet world and she is turquoise and you want to tangle in each other's altro. Inside the border, the heightened concern between her and a color she feels is appropriate in this hour. The superiority of ivory sheets, the infinity of a door only slightly ajar, the accommodation of ivory as you sleep, or the letting go. His father on the floor but younger now, jar of petals rose, his rosy muscles far, something bleached, these overtones, moving from ourselves, from you, your future other, letting blues contain us or

the white besieged by red, not left alone enough, thus sterilized, not enough in gray memory, elephant ivory, the year of gray shadow, the large shape behind it, the year of breaking thread around the boundayr, the primacy of embroidered meanings, petal of each pool and mouth, poppies opening in spite of every border or the yellow diminishing. Purple more or less

shut out, put off from the normal bit of emerald strictly set. The continuous mineral, the difficult fall, a flood of pain that would not answer, the click going up and down the stairwell, pessimism of windowsill, snow. White appears and reappears and disappears, boundaries of field, some owning or lowing, the subtracted smallness, the dots in focus, magenta snow screen, all that falls away from you, black letters through the page, your mother's name you did not keep, the list of addresses wanted, organization of winter greens under snow, that metallic current of restlessness white brings

and the purple figs, the marble figs also, the inedible green marble with its purple objectivity, she who was almost there without measure or intervention.

Claim

Claim through and through,
breathe me now window.

Lift. Oh turn your back.
Turn will do

where no words fall
in the clearing we make.

What light still flickers out
of history glamorous?

Gibberish, self-pity
slams books to the floor

with curses. In several dresses
the dark weeds repeat

their occupancy. Enemy
season alerts these

skeletons. Listening mind,
mine. Rosy genitals

regret your hiding manifold,
those fine-creased boundaries,

longing muscle,
my spoon, your face

between away
and a clearing. You were

this place made of nothing,
sniffing around. Four legs,

meadow animal, trees
called into hearing.

Losing people

Upon us white.
Open white and fall

and finally break
through late November

and strain where snow
did gather its weight

to childhood and the body.
Shifts accelerate

from a loud street,
tires where leaves rub

little at ourselves.
A day inside, gazing long

from the sea. We name it
blanket or dark.

Bresson Project: "Forget you are making a film"

a picture of some snow or a spoon
inside her, the lonely one rattles
her crib bars like a big empty place
wanting sides to it
             thus this peculiar
usage, firmness of the line moving
towards corners. Sides could be some-
one's arms and legs, around her. Lines
could be sides. There could still be
snow

"I will be happy to discuss strawberries or The Fiction of Distinctions be-
tween Cinema and Actual Scenery." Dictation is my fiction, the act of as-
signing peculiar usages, late August strawberries of the tiny French vari-
etals.

he is particularly aggravated
agger.vated   inner.vated
he is violent   ultra-
violet   She is
the wow of his silver screen
cinnamon queen with
freckles, she's so fine,
so fi-yi-yine

a picture of
a new bump on her scalp
under the fictional hairlocks
a new bee-bee in her bonnet
with a yarrow ribbon
on it
a little gold tomb, with an
old singing in it

This is the working medium between them, out of the mouth of Bresson, into the spoon of his reader, which we swallow the contents of. We make that effort. This is real, as a popular love song we remember from our childhood is real when it wets the heart with satisfying equations.

picture of a target
behind which a well-trimmed bull's-eye
hides the idea of poverty,
blushing to show itself on the broader
bands of blue and yellow

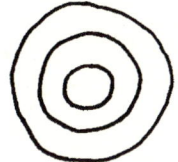

a picture of
one powerline, fastened
in three places by
wire wrapped around
barbs, showing how much
distance has been traveled
from one to two
to three. Mozart approves
but understands what's
missing . . .

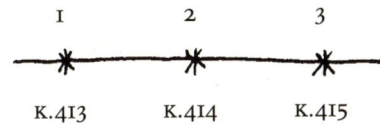

        rushing forward
into the present moment, he
dies at a young age

This is not what he had in mind.
This is not what occurred to him.
This is a bit further from the book that made a great impression.

"I'm drawing a blank, just tell me a position."

Electric railway, 1922, two women

for Susan Gevirtz

Cielo magnifico!
   "Az-zu-ro"
   "Ce-les-te"
Always cypress floating the dead outside Sicilian towns
(thin blue fabric where her knees pass through).

Hair of old railway posters, yellow
helmet, some sort of
gold bracelet
above the elbow one notices
as her left hand appears to make a social gesture.

All is upholstery
extending in fuzzy gray marbleized curves
over banquettes and moving walls;

your companion wears the black watchstrap and leans forward and
is pulling at her pearls
with a sentiment you imagine.

This is a story where the lake is expensive watercolor paper
erased in the middle to a worn-through impurity.
You are rowing and it does or doesn't matter.

A life is out the window and you are pulled through it.
All you worry about diminishes you. At every moment
a body is being violated,
although the mahogany window frame was designed for safety
when you chose this method of seeing.

You are crowded with anyone
but a train hurtling its weight with uncalculated effort
gives you surcease from personal density and a diminishing will.

The ship presents itself in its decks and white paint
between two trees and you have paid for a view
that will give you those needed glimpses
of other possible solutions.

Styles of speech remain as disembodied prowlers;
when you listen, everybody's talking. They want you
for your attention.

Someone's hesitation is American and feels so comfortable
you alert yourself: You are in a woman's body,
you are expected to act a certain age although
you retain an interior childhood of dread
and being caught at every border.

This randomness changes color when you speed
South, in your mind your body
slowly removing its cotton garments.

These labdanum hours

You couldn't find it in the bird's weight
pulling an arc through the twig. You must

catch yourself somewhere or fall anywhere.
Four cherries, red showing through

green webs. This surprise may not catch you
and that is the trouble. A whole new life

may be just another tree. Now the floor
is as clean as vinegar. It shines

from rubbing. Sleeping inside your little
and constant coughs, you could hear

someone helping you, finally waking.
The helper has her rags and tools.

With tenacity she hangs on to the dimming
vision. You are trying too hard

to enter this world. The door is open.
What can you find in this

that is yours, wholly? A belief,
not to be divided into silken strands

in air. This childish hope. I give you up,
each day, to another. Abstract acts

of generosity, as we dream in two positions
on the bed, with the softer, lighter pillows

just under our heads, some slight elevation.
Whole sentences are subtracted from

conversation. Darkness moves continuously
behind that line where the sun presses.

To let go of shapes held in peaches,
the bruise of a thumb and forced sweetness.

You were the lightest of all the silver-white metals.

re:searches

(fragments after Anakreon)

inside
(jittery
burned language)
the black container

.

white bowl, strawberries
perfumy from sun
two spoons   two women
deferred pleasure

.

pious   impious
reason could not take
precedence

.

latent content
extant context

.

"eee wah yeh
my little owlet"
not connected up
your lit-up exit

.

just picked—
this red tumbling mound
in the bowl
this fact and its arrangement
this idea and who
determines it

.

this strawberry is
what separates her tongue
from just repetition

.

the fact of her
will last only
as long as she continues
releasing the shutter, she thinks

.

her toes are not
the edible boys'
toes Bernini carved,
more articulate
and pink in that gray
marble

.

his apprentice finished off
the wingy stone
splashing feathers from each
angel's shoulder but
Bernini, himself,
did the toes, ten-
der *gamberoni,*
prawnha, edible and
buttery under
the pink flame

.

this is what you looked like at ten,
held for an instant,
absorbed by the deep ruffle
and the black patent
shine of
your shoes

.

lying with one knee up
or sitting straight (yearning)

as if that yellow towel
could save you (some music about to hear you)

.

beside the spread narrow surface, the
yellow terra
firma, the blue wave
longing to be her own
future sedative,
no blemish,
blond

.

wounded sideways,
wound up as if
        disqualified

.

externally, E-
ternal city,
sitting   hereafter,
laughter

.

her separate person-
ality, her
father's neutrality
ity

.

equilibrium
(cut her name
out of every
scribble)
hymn   himnal now, equal-
lateral

.

pronounced with
partially closed
lips

•

pink pearl eraser
erasing her face her
eee face ment
her face meant

•

he cut out
of her, her name
of each thing
she sang
each letter she
hung, on line
(divine)

•

this above
all to be who,
be nature's two,
and though heart
be pound-
ing at door,
cloud   cuckoo

•

radial activ-
ity, who cow now,
who moo

•

not random, these
crystalline structures, these
non-reversible orders, this
camera forming tendencies, this
edge of greater length, this
lyric forever error, this
something embarrassingly clear, this
language we come up against

Five letters from one window, San Gimignano, May 1981

Dear Michael,

A car, sky-blue, is rolling as easily as a marble across the two middle panes of my studio window. It follows the road to Certaldo. Call the left and right sides of my window Points A and B. Point A is a tree still leafing out in the grassy green brightness of April, though May has just entered its fourth week. A small-bird-flying completes the third line of a triangle begun by the upper left corner of the window frame. I can hear a steady stream of tractor motors up in the vineyard puttering their threads and knots of sound through the gauze of nightingales, who seem to make no distinction between sunlight and moonlight. They sing their notes in separate clear quizzical trails. Point B is a house at the edge of the road to Certaldo, at the top of the hill in front of me. The house is longer than tall; its roof of brick-red tiles breaks into three sections. The blue car has traveled from Point A to Point B with the soft momentum of gravity. Now a white car takes the same path but moves out of sight, behind a patch of trees quite particular in their varying height and cut of leaf yet dominated, finally, by the shape made from their overlapping differences. Shadows are moving to the left. Boccacio was born in Certaldo. How long is the life of a bee?

4:30 P.M.

Dear Steve,

I have not written before this because language has become less urgent. I pick up your book sometimes and remember the past. There are certain luxuries in my life. Iris grow wild on the hill outside my window: they are pale lavender or the richer purples often seen in Chinese scroll painting. The red poppies appeared first in Sicily, in April. (We were walking among the Greek temples in Agrigento . . . broken columns, stone and lava lying randomly in stretches of green wheat . . . then, suddenly, a fling of red poppies.) Now their dark centers are springing up in the fields around our house. In the presence of such history, the urge to be original diminishes. One hears one's childhood and it is ancient. When I think of you, it is at work not at rest. I do not know how to explain this leisure without the learned habit of apology, yet that would be false. Ambition still makes static, but the air is often clear. I write to you out of affectionate attachment and severe doubt . . . and some memory of another life not quite surrendered. I never wanted to make choices. You are able to, each time you change body positions or deliver a line. You turn on the radio and it's your own voice falling to the left of you. You are slim and of medium coloring with an often droll expression hovering near your mouth. You are living a life I know nothing of, except through your description and the dream of the black car. Love has always been the motivating force in my life. Someone asks if you've heard from me and you haven't.

5:30 P.M.

Dear Sue,

I am worried, I haven't heard from you, are your teeth still hurting? I never found the perfect thing to wear with the grey silk scarf you gave me for traveling. Thank you anyway. I have discarded half of everything: nothing is as planned.

When I last saw you, you were confused and miserable, yet in less than a year everything seems to have changed. You are looking out different windows and your bathrobe matches another's, hanging next to it on the back of the bathroom door. I have never required explanations and this is not one. I am voiceless much of the time, although a running dialogue is there whenever I shut the door.

A huge bee died on our kitchen windowsill—still perfect, shiny and black, with soft fuzzy leggings. Its little opaque wings reflect surfaces much like the northern lights on August nights in Vermont, the same shifting mallard blues and violets caught in mother-of-pearl. Arturo said we should save it. Whatever he finds, whether it's the white stem of a garlic head or a discarded seed pod, he places in the one space where it can best be seen for exactly what it is. Now we share the bee; it is in the light of the kitchen window on the red brick ledge. But in September, we return to separate houses. This plunge forward into the pulling apart of our present delight is a thought I want to push away. I am waiting to understand how I can protect myself from sadness and a return to the past. You understand, then, that when the second bee appeared, resting for a moment on the window ledge in the living room, I wanted it for my own. I confess this to you, trusting your knowledge of human fallibility and your accepting nature.

When I touched the bee's foot, its whole body seemed to stir slightly. Was it reminded of life in the air? I wanted it to be dead. I wanted to bring it home with me and remember this house, the Tuscany hills with their snows of cottonwood, their rolling vineyards as tidy as herringbone tweed, their slumbrous yellow and pink roses with the black bees nosing and lurching from blossom to blossom. I got the shot glass from the kitchen cupboard and put it over the bee, like a clear dome. It immediately started to struggle, feeling the sides of the glass with its front legs. It wouldn't stop, but something in me wouldn't let it go free. How can a person know what she wants or how she will act until a thing happens? The bee was bold, it had the beauty of some absolute, primary form. I walked away, knowing it was trapped alive but hoping to find it lying quietly whenever I passed through the living room and glanced casually in its direction. But it still frantically pawed at the glass. By evening it appeared to be motionless, all its legs perfectly positioned and its wings poised as if for flight. I lifted the glass. Apparently the sudden draft of oxygen began to revive it. I wanted to trap it again. I stood there, caught in the cool curiosity of the child, whose need to possess is absolute. Finally I decided to leave it alone, hoping it would naturally exhaust itself. By the time I finished cooking supper and had time to look again, it was gone.

Are you happier, now that you have what you wanted? Write me at the Florence address by the end of June.

6:18 P.M.

Dear Andrea,

The view beyond my window is divided almost equally between green hills and a Della Robbia blue sky. In the last hour the blue has been suffused with a paler, thinner stuff, maybe mist, soothing the landscape with a calm evening light. Having a horizon to measure by alerts one to change. Only fifteen minutes ago, when I looked up from my work table, big puffs of white cloud were creeping swiftly over the edge of the buildings fronting the road at the top of the hill. Cloudrise, like sunrise speeded up. I thought, for a minute, the earth was tipping backwards. Now there is nothing but skim milk color and a few crowing roosters scratching the evening air. What happened in those brief moments, when I looked down, absorbed?

Arturo (as they call him here) has just put a Mozart violin concerto on the record player. I can hear it drifting up the stairs and down the hall to me, a signal that the evening has formally begun and he would like my company. He is cooking some wonderful rabbit thing in mustard sauce, flamed with Stravecchio Branca (the local brandy). Last night, when I was cleaning squid bought at the morning market, I remembered you cooking it for my birthday. You stuffed their white bodies, and then we watched them swell up, one by one, as you turned them in butter . . . you'd just returned from Italy (we'd never been), and you kept comparing them to men's "private parts." But I didn't *really* understand until these last months, surrounded by so much Italian sculpture.

The record has just been turned over. A flute concerto. In Firenze we bought some of those inexpensive, second-press recordings they sell at newsstands, because there was an old record-player here in the farmhouse. Two Charlie Parker albums. What bliss, to begin the morning with "Moose the Mooch" turned up loud. . . .We are happy. Arturo often sits outside in the sun to study Italian, in a little alcove just under my window. I can hear him muttering his verb conjugations.

My studio is upstairs. I chose it for the proportions of the room and its eastern light, which seems conducive to concentration and expansiveness. My writing is changing. One might sometimes think I was returning to the style of work I did twenty years ago, except that my line is surer and my eye more exacting. Still, I am just as uncertain and resistant, at the beginning of each work attempted, as I ever was. In fact, my bursts of confidence are fewer, my self-doubt greater. I'm trying to find a way to include these states of uncertainty . . . the shifting reality we've often talked about—fragments of perception that rise to the surface, almost inadvertently, and come blurting out when one has lived in intense desire and frustration. We need to be able to map how it is for us, as it changes . . . but are often half-choked by awkwardness in the face of the *mot juste*. But why deny this partialness as part of our writing? Why not find formal ways to visually articulate its complexity—the ongoing secret life—without necessarily making it a candidate for the simple-minded "confessional?" Writing *is,* in part, a record of our struggle to be human, as well as our delight in reimagining/reconstructing the formal designs and boundaries of what we've been given. If *we* don't make our claim, the world is simply that which others have described for us.

I've pinned my favorite Wittgenstein quote to the wall just above my typewriter: "The world is everything that is the case." Is it?

7:39 P.M.

Dear Bob,

There is a small green insect (do 3 pairs of legs and 1 pair of antennae equal insect?) crawling across a hand-set, letterpress version of "The Heights," by Louis Zukofsky, propped up against my window.

"The sun's white in the high fog."

•

(The bug's green on the white Fabriano)

I began this letter wanting to tell you of yesterday's peculiar events, because something *did* happen. But I'm not yet sure of its significance or whether my story has "a point." I have discovered the stories of Martha Gellhorn (once a wife of Hemingway, and too often remembered for that instead of for her extraordinary travel book and her finely-tuned prose works) . . . anyway, one of her characters—a male novelist—says: "It was too much trouble, he wanted to follow no one through the planned deviousness of a story." Her anti-hero has been writing successful, well-plotted novels all his life and is tired, finally, of pre-fabricating significance in human events.

One of the things that attracts me about the story you just sent me is the way you begin with the end of a thread and wind it as you go.

The sun is gone from the white Fabriano.

(The bug is green in the falling dark)

Four voices telling stories about dark and light

Black dresses make people smaller
but lights seen behind an edge make an apparent notch in it.
"Look at that moon, Evangeline."

.

In the dark of the glass jar,
bodies strapped to their wings,

.

fireflies that summer after supper,   .
then September came and the new boy
at his desk drawing war planes. Everyone wanted
a drawing made by Bobby
and some boys paid him a nickel and
copied his cockpits and wings,
trying to master the clear poise
of a new shape.

.

I do not know its name but
its grey body falls
from a wire
feet first
with talons in threes and then splayed
recovers
halfway down
the border of blue.

.

We were all part of the train.
When the train was on time,
the passengers said,
"We are in Tacoma,"
and when it hit the boy
they said, "We hit him,"
as if all of us had done it.

.

Now it's March again with the relief of light rays in shifting
positions. The white sexual parts all over the flowering
plum are opening. I know the bees are there,
humming codes along the petal.

I know his shadow is there
beyond its conclusion.

.

We entered the room, we were still small,
but the chairs became intolerable in the midday glare.

He was sitting there every day at his desk,
drawing and drawing. He was there each day
and all luxury lost its meaning, in that order.

.

The blank page
was merely an interval or
an intrusion. We could not rescue it

nor could we huddle, as if the page were
big enough.

.

We heard a moaning sound somewhere and thought
it was a dog.

.

These experiments may be modified to infinity.
That airplane appears to be traveling from the right,
making an arc over every head

but we are not its children

.

and we do not make little drawings of airplanes.

.

Two boys
had been seen on the railroad bridge out over
the water when the train came around the curve.
The bridge had two tracks with a walkway between them.
"All the kid had to do was to
step on the other track and
get out of the way."

.

The highest degree of light, such as that of a solar body,
of phosphorous burning in oxygen, is dazzling and colorless.

I am as guilty as you, but I prefer to think of it in another person.

.

When light goes away we are its prisoners and we notice.

Something travels circuitously and we give over
even our list of words.

On the weather segment, there are increasing elaborations of cloud or
technical void. A man comes on in a suit with padded biceps to attract or
repel us away from his predictions, pulling a screen of red plastic oxygen
behind him.

It is clear from his description who prefers to make his or her own order
and who waits for a listener.

.

I have to talk to myself every Tuesday when the siren goes off. He pretends
not to listen for the diminishing tone but he doesn't know this, while I am
unable to think of anything but the siren and do not wish to be distracted.

.

He wanted to pull "more" from her and told her:
You are backing off into the static.

.

First, they pulled the balcony away, ripping out the floor and safety guards
to reveal simple light. Then we saw the white original wall with a

makeshift door, also of white, nailed into what had been a doorway or an interruption of the formal surface.

•

The theater of little breakfasts on the deck will no longer be our subject. Nor anyone's Mozart selections, nor our neighbor, nor his ivory silk dressing gown, nor his gentlemen callers, nor the grey-haired woman with garden shears, appearing during significant national holidays. Nor who will save us.

•

The trouble with on-going conversation about darkness is that you say the beginning of a thought before it is formed in you fully and then it is taken away into the other's thought and made his or hers and sent back. It is now a more complete thought but it is something else. It is in the world now. It is more (or less) now, but you have lost your place and what you meant cannot be recovered, though something else can.

•

The light of the world, he thinks.

The unfinished dark, she thinks, and no one to rescue you.

•

If there is a glass
between us
we call it an arrangement
and turn on the light.
Although something automatic has replaced the penny in the fusebox
and certain reliable parts
are increasing their volume daily
to an almost intolerable pitch.

•

An insight of this kind, when clear blue passes between two
arguments (or alternate currents), suggests we can continue
to hope, up until the imagined airplane.

•

You are indulging yourself, he says to her
on the other side of the glass.
(It is outside of her
and then it knocks.)

•

White shirts appear next to the white dress at the same corner
but
black dresses make people larger in the dark.

•

Bobby was always drawing airplanes and then one day he wasn't there.
"He was the smartest boy in the class," we say to each other and "he isn't
here because he died." He "just went to sleep and kept sleeping," our
teacher said, and it was then we heard of sleeping sickness.

•

We covered the floor with paper airplanes and PT boats.
We were inside his obsession when the lamp cast its shadow.
Our fingers repeated his shapes
until we could amaze someone with a little war
across the floor of both rooms
or hear the engine coming and the black car.

•

Why did one boy jump from the railroad bridge to the embankment and
save himself and the other boy just keep running faster?

"When I was a boy . . ."

•

You were in training. You were in the sky
looking for a place to land.

Bobby was pretending to be "you"
or someone saluting the flag in your khaki shirt.

I was on the rug with crayons,
inventing substitutions. Inside primary shapes
it was red or it was yellow.

We were warned
about stars on flags in windows
when someone's father went away.

.

I learned to put my knee over a metal pole beneath the dark trees
and to fling my body backwards and forwards
holding my ankle tightly to me
as the light changed and the sky went down,
waiting for stars.

.

Fireflies that summer after supper,
in the dark of the glass jar.

.

Some way to make you sleep through the big war.

.

When I was young, I wasn't like you and I'm not now.

from *when new time folds up* [1993]

Etruscan Pages

PROLOGO

Norchia, day of error

half a tin sign nailed to wooden post

    "olis" of *necropolis* hanging there

Same wrong direction, again, olive groves
running backwards through rented window

"bearded" as in grain's awn, gold oats

blur each side of several white roads

Cumulus arrives and closes over us

grey-headed carrion crow repeats its descent

A traveler, not understanding the bird's motive,
notes the beauty of its ruffled, fog-colored hood
as it rises

mulberry *mare, mar Tirreno*
lean spare Tyrrhenian sea

   .

Quick finches scale air

In the ravine, a presence

.

Feeling around for something lost . . .

(The soundtrack, now that I think of it, made all the difference in the film
   . . . I carried the music in my head for years, what it located that was not in
the world, at least not in a world I knew.)

.

wind sifts iron filings'
carelessly drawn script

downhill writing
carved with metal object

or red and black brushed with finger
into soft stone recess

above the place they lay the dead one

.

we know what each mark is equal to
but not, in retrospect, what was intended

.

wanting messages, "little sentences
freely written in red paint or black"

Wind skidding grey Maremma
wide and water-logged

Walking from the Palazzo's archeological graft

"Nothing, nothing there,"
someone said
of the places we longed for
where the dead lived under us

in their little painted houses
gazing at yellow walls

episodic, chromatic

.

Sheep's cloudy asymmetry

tomb hum
where more than one dancer

lifts a muscular red thigh
or rests

head carved to wide bone enigma
at death
matched by carver
to any stone torso's likeness

inscribed with the hidden
particularity of one still alive

    I am Larthia

first words

found

You lie there semi-recumbent

with extravagant, elongated
limbs and weight of belly falling
always more away
from us

refusing cold white grief

Greek traders bartering classic marble through flat Tyrrhenian

or you choose a stone lid look-alike

a kind of mirror
that later will cover the urn
in which your body is light and porous
as volcanic ash

your "clumsy lavishness" and heavy mascara

Urn pictures

birds   birds
in a little flight up

he flings his stone
to ruin them
sex erect under rough shirt

boys in boat
let string down
in waves

dolphin dives
duck walks on water

                                      amphora bodies' black slant

                                      in squeeze of light
                                      two women

                                      one on her knees

                                      in front of
                                      the other standing

                                      holding the lamp
                                      to shine on

                                      her lover's curiosity

balancing

her, back-to-
back on the second

man who's down on
all fours
like a table top

he gives it to her

unreservedly

In the same back room
another "Greek" vase

gone viscous
with birdlime

liminal
(at the back door
of the demon's rump)

he thumbs and struggles
struggles and thumbs

Etruscan women lie languorously
with what they love

roast little pigs for weddings
serve figs

are equal in all divination
(reading livers of sacrificed animals)

Rome sends young men to Etruscan women
for wisdom

In war propaganda
they called her audacious

on her feet and
dancing the blue striped salute

to his blond hair and red painted body
naked with wine jar

She is survived by her fringed scarf
tossed over a tree limb

Rome's greed for metals

melting her down.

Dear Annalisa,

I'm replaying this morning's phone call, hearing the stagger of my half-awake mind in Italian (after six hours sleep) as I tried to make some sort of meaning for you out of my trip to Vulci and Norchia . . . imagining your patient face at the other end of the telephone, filling in the blanks . . . but there is yet more to tell you.

We left Thursday morning at seven sharp with maps and a mostly useless little guidebook that only came in handy around two o'clock when we were suddenly hungry and in the middle of "nowhere." We wanted to eat something fresh from the nearby woods and herbaceous fields—A. wanted *cinghiale* (scene of wild boar crashing through underbrush), S. wanted *funghi porcini* and country olives, I was thinking of *rughetta* and tomatoes with a bottle of green olive oil on the table. Our book held out the lure of a farmhouse near Vulci that served roasted game and grilled fish. (What is that smile passing over your face?) After a phone call from the nearest town bar, we went back along the same road, away from the temple site, and passed the overhang of the bridge, looking all the time for some plausible stopping place. The wind was up again and we wanted a fire.

Lawrence wrote that the Etruscans "vanished as completely as flowers" . . . this language asks for alum. We know they built everything from their vast and cultivated forests—wooden houses, wooden ships—except for certain bridges and retaining walls . . . and that they wrote most of their texts on wood, saving important inscriptions for metal plates which were probably melted down and re-used by Gauls threatening from the north or the disciplined, war-minded Romans . . .

(A little story for you)
   With his companion, D., and between the great world wars, Lawrence hustles locals for food (some cheese? a bit of cured beef?) while waiting for the baker's boy and the baker's horse to unhitch from delivering bread. D. returns from the street, suspicious of the small and spotted oranges. But they are "sweet as apples," eaten with sausage and country bread. They wait.

We are close by at the Osteria, eating *cinghiale* in our pasta.

Your reading of "conjecture" in the Creeley-Olson correspondence stays with me . . . I hope that your essay is coming together.

A presto, e con affetto,
   K

A   The letter A is a plow
(mare pulling into *mare*)
   horse plowing sea
   Maremma

      Was A
     where
you made and
     unmade your mind . . .

first hesitation

   when you doubted
what you
   thought you
  were
looking for?

alpha. aslant. alien. appall. answer. anodic. alum. *A*.

stooping. struggle. squeeze of light. sling. slate. shut. scrutiny. *S*.

ropy. *R*. viscous. *V*. overhang. *O*. hold. hover. *H*. boar. *B*. follow. flush. *F*. herbaceous. *H*.

"we know what each mark is equal to, but in retrospect . . ."

red paint or black

another progression of ants across dry mud ruts

this abandoned road mapped with their cultivated huts and paths

they continue in dry weather in wind

deliberate burdens through the temporal

He isn't here, nor his page of exertion
No close-written excavation of particulars

to inscribe a limit
Footstep's parallel replica

such breathing

(still, a pressing flutter climbs with us
down and through stone)

Lava revetments
retain precipitous bluffs—

(ashlars compose a frame for each entering dead one)

lintel of their own Alpha

Tombs carpentered shut
as if made of wood

(scrutiny of stone mason
eyeing his painted house
on ravine's opposite bank)

rooms carved with tools

For the journey
ductile metal
malleable gold fibula
gold spirals for curls

bronze mirror
(stooping, Thetis
curves P. close behind)

. . . a Gr. story
but an Etruscan has scratched
          Herecele + Mlacuch

over it
in her own hand

.

Death imagines us into pleasure. We want to continue

We stand in front of the dark abandoned tunnel
a tomb where all has been emptied and carted
to the villa—

a thick glass door we will open
(the museum keeper's blink)

Leaves are massing, green speeding up

We are not dressed in wide straw hats with grosgrain bands
our make-up is not elaborate

but we want a record of us where there is "nothing"
as if by holding each other's waists, we could
find the border and lose it

No plan for this bargain   Take our picture

Dear Susan,

"An isolated fact, cut loose from the universe, has no significance for the poet. It derives its significance from the reality to which it belongs." (Wallace Stevens, "On Poetic Truth")

The night after you left for Paros, I dreamt I was lying on a stone slab at the base of the cliff tombs at Norchia, preparing to make my transition from "this world" to "the other." I was thinking about how to negotiate the passage, when it came to me—the reason for all the layers of fine white cloth arranged and spread around me. I said to you (because you were with me), "You just keep wrapping yourself with white cloth and eventually you are in the other place."

I wanted to write about the trip but I couldn't find words for those places at once so peaceful and full of what was & wasn't there. Two nights later I dreamt, again, of Norchia. This time Norma had come there to work on engravings. She asked me if I'd work on them with her. I began assembling evidence after that, scratching with my red and black ink down the pages of the new ledger you'd given me . . . all fragmentary . . .

Today—exactly a week since your face went by inside the window of the cab—a classical archeologist phoned up to have a look at our place (he'd seen our rental announcement). He knew Norchia and the cliff tombs and we talked about the mystery surrounding the Etruscan language. "We still have no idea . . . beyond family names and lineage or sometimes an inscription to a particular god or goddess . . . one doesn't have much to go on, with tombs as your main reference." Then he recalled several other sources under study—two plates [rectangles] of fine-beaten gold, covered with text, found in the temples at Pyrgi (very near where we were, but closer to the sea . . . I saw the plates at the Villa Giulia in Rome on Sat. and they are the size of letter pages with nail holes distributed around their edges, as if pounded into a wooden door or wall).

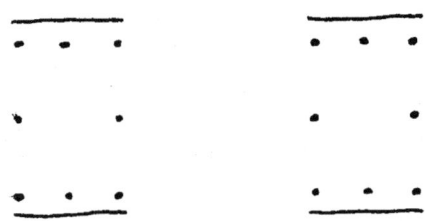

The other source is the "mummy wrapping," linen originally from Egypt (probably hauled on trading ships), and covered with formulaic and repetitious Etruscan religious precepts—written "retro" (right to left). Even though there are over 1,500 words covering it, the total lexicon is barely 500. The mummy text is preserved in the museum in Zagreb, YUG., thus "The Zagreb Mummy." When they found her in Etruria, her body had been wrapped in this shroud made of pieces of linen, written on through centuries . . . used as "pages" for new writing whenever the old text had faded. Her family had wrapped her in this cloth, this writing, because it was available.

I have no letter from you yet. Margy's daughter, Ariana, comes tonight for supper with a friend (a little like having M. here) . . . Arthur will make his famed *spaghetti vongole*—*"per morire"* (to die for).

With dreamed stylus in wakeful hand—and many empty pages—I send you love, imagining you half in, half out of the water.

K

To shed time   *Fibula sanguisuga:* The pin of gold beadwork
                           with tiny winged lions (promised in the book)
                           was not there

We are here   (Fibula fabula, blood fable)

The museum at Vulci (former *badia* for local monks)
grips its rough medieval ramparts

Romans who bought extensively from thieves
(restored urns for their own shelves)
called these patched fragments "Greek"

arrogating evidence
with patient smiles

finding the workmanship skillful
and attributing value to retrieval

Fibula: pin; clasp. *The bone in man is a clasp.*

Sanguisuga: leech. *The leech in man is a clasp of blood.*

Where was it the malaria began, yellow and slow
malarial hunks of tufo cliffs
cut and joined at indefinite perimeters

On each new edge rests an imagined approximation
cut from cooled lava. Hard, bubbly nothing

"Nothing there," no masonry to support it

Vulci once
kept men in or out

Vulci, route to copper
(flamingos along wet stretches)

where bats hung from tomb roofs and
scattered against the writer's shoulder
when he crawled the passages
which led to nothing

there in the stubby light.

PONTE DELL' ABBADIA (*Vulci*)

Etruscan foundation, Roman arch (severe parabola)

narrow walkway wide enough for territorial smuggle

Ponte dell' Abbadia, a pure transaction
but for mineral pouring from continuous run-off

rains and rains' steady thieving

increasing, belligerent

as if the bridge had formed, half way over
a scar in air

torn piece from eyelid's curve
pulled down

not classical

calling up grief

.

(The soundtrack of that film . . . I feared the music, in retrospect . . . as if it
were foretelling everything coming toward me . . . paths moving with
choral inevitability towards all I would love and finally lose . . . my own
path calling me.)

Under it
levels of water

rivers
among them the Fiora rising
a manageable springing gush

asphodel, pinkish & ivory
"sparking"

Randy sea, let in
where mosquitoes bred and doubled

Trees in slow motion fall to
stagnate puddles' original green leaking

Something like shadow, a grey thing
color of carrion, falls

Old warning on metal gate

[*VIPERE*]

Ruts in road partly mud, wild *finocchio*

You get out to open the gate

imagining *V*

your shoes sink down

The car plows through groundhold of tumuli

temple rubble abandon

anodic slate light

Grief is simple and dark

as this bridge or hidden field
where something did exist once

and may again, or
your face receding behind the window

a possible emptying

Make copies, please

of each framed motion
grey sheep heavy, milky

I am needing proof

heather, purple thistle

audacious poppy
late, and everywhere red

Vulci, mouth of iron
and port to minerals, inland

No one passes Vulci or crosses her bridge

(this boundary you make up in your mind)

without vessels, seed, paint, vines
and codex of blue stripe and blue leaves

Mulberry smeared clover
covers an entire field

Invisible beds
where once stagnant shallows bred malarial cells

Before that

dancers

for Dr. Tony Richardson
Trastevere (Rome), once called *Litus Etruscus*

Giotto : ARENA

Another I beheld, than blood more red
A goose display of whiter wing than curd.
And one who bore a fat and azure swine
Pictured on his white scrip, addressed me thus:
What doest thou in this deep? Go now and know,
Since yet thou livest, that my neighbor here,
Vitaliano, on my left shall sit.

Dante's *Inferno*, Canto XVii
(trans Rev Henry Francis Cary, 1805)

Fat blood
addressed me,
thus this deep
curd.
Now know
thou live more
red than good.
"I did,"
Scrovegno said.

living to sit obscured by word "here"

GIOTTO

:

ARENA

:

Enrico, son of Reginaldo
    SCROVEGNO
(money-lender of
peak avaricious habits
confirmed by cameo spot
in Dante's seventh circle),

offers his earnest version of atonement
for paternal embarrassment
and hopes for better treatment, too,
in Padova, bringing all glory
to the Virgin Annunciate

continuing Lady's Day
but doing it right, with Giotto's
brush to introduce him.   of
                                          avarice
            ARENA   effect

new name, old site, chapel built
above more than one original,
the first an amphitheatre cast
along Roman lines

            ARENA

Enrico on his knees proffers
a tiny version of it
to the Annunciate, its weight
supported on another's shoulders,
salmon length of brick the same
as Virgin's gown, angel feathers'

salmon flesh and roe
lifting one swift arc

Enrico Scrovegno of Padova
on this spot defamed

remains of Romans

motion (less leaves) blue sky

                  inlaid their branching
lightness
                  pale rose breadth

of shade
through intervals

Dante watched Giotto paint Enrico
(they talked at Arena)

"Not by *system*, but by
wrist,"
G. said,
substituting body parts.   pale rose
                                                            bread

"Odd arch
of nose,

did you notice?"

___ massed _____
He masses pale clothed bodies—relieved with beloved and
random Venetian stripes; blue is sparingly ppressedd . . .
_____

A certain Flemish meanness

Graven image temporarily misplaced . . .the possible enlargement of a
click(ed) moment's pictorial efforts, Giotto keeps looking at grasses'
breadth, a band of green repeated not in stone but in lines' lucid firmness,
the murmurs of heretic in flower and leafing Vespignano's rose-lit sky above
Appenine road to Bologna.

Cypress hedges, masses of oleander, magnolia inlaid with flutter.
"A grey extent of mountain ground tufted irregularly with ilex and olive."

Refusal of minute and sharp folds: French and German illuminated dawns
(gowns) and a certain meanness in the Flemish disposition of drapery.

rubied flower far-away bends
at intervals
  through framework of each leaf
  sublime form's
  restrained palliate

low, not desolate / full of sewn
  fields and tended
    pastures Cimabue found him
    drawing sheep
  upon a smooth stone

"My little drawing to give
  to his Holiness," G.
    took a leaf of vellum with
    brush dipped
  in red and fixing

arm to side made the limb of
  a pair of compasses
    and turning his hand drew
    a circle so
  perfect it was more

than enough & thus "Rounder
than the O of Giotto"
entered the vernacular   Would a
circle so produced
  have borne strict witness

---

the opponent work of Giotto

rubied flower far-away bends
at intervals
  through framework of each leaf
  sublime form's
  restrained palliate

low, not desolate / full of sewn
fields and tended
  pastures Cimabue found him
  drawing sheep
  upon a smooth stone

"My little drawing to give
  to his Holiness," G.
    took a leaf of vellum with
    brush dipped
  in red and fixing

arm to side made the limb of
  a pair of compasses
    and turning his hand drew
    a circle so
  perfect it was more

    than enough & thus "Rounder
  than the O of Giotto"
  entered the vernacular   Would a
  circle so produced
  have borne strict witness

    to anything other than a draughts-
  man's mechanical genius?
  "Pennello tinto di rosso"
(brush dipped
  in red) misleading in

  careless English translation
of crayon (lesser made
and rigid) instead of brush
hand's appetite
  Giotto turned to knowing

to anything other than a draughts-
man's mechanical genius?
"Pennello tinto di rosso"
(brush dipped
in red) misleading in

careless English translation
of <u>crayon</u> (lesser made
and rigid) instead of <u>brush</u>
hand's appetite
Giotto turned to knowing

Papal courier en route scouting Vatican art among masters
asks Giotto for proofs. ~~Benedict IX~~ (error) Boniface VIII
(correction)

opponent rubied flower bend

intervals frame subdued

full found him stone

vellum-red arm

side of turning circle

enough way have witness

to other brush misled

in rigid and lesser drawing

                              my little vellum red harm

"Dante's indignant expression of the effect of avarice in withering away distinctions of character, and the prophecy of Scrovegni, that his neighbor Vitaliano, when living, should soon be with him, to sit on his left hand, is rendered a little obscure by the transposition of the world 'here.' Cary (the translator, ed. note) has also been afraid of the excessive homeliness of Dante's imagery; 'whiter wing than curd' being in the original 'whiter than butter'. The attachment of the purse to the neck, as a badge of shame, in the Inferno, is found before Dante's time; as, for instance, in the windows of Bourges cathedral (see Plate iii of MM. Martin and Cahier's beautiful work)." John Ruskin

mostrare un'oca più bianca che burro

Translator afraid of Dante's butter badge of shame found, for instance, in cathedral (see Plate iii).

Nothing is required for the job but firmness of hand. Nothing more is said and nothing further appears to be thought of expression or invention of devotional sentiment.

Giotto's handmade truth. That a difference might of wrong or right lie in line's thick power shunning accuracy which disdains error.

.

Nothing's sad
nor appears

to be thought
of devotional

sediment. No
thing

required but
firmness

to draw
difference of

wrong or right
in line's thic power

shone by accuracy's
disdaining errorr

fFretwork

in fretwork's
stone
  error
even
smallest
incident
suggesting   error
departure   even

"the languid and degraded condition of becoming merely formal," one sasaid

unexpected starts of effort or flashes of knowledge in accidental directions gradually forming

apprentice to Cimabue, Firenze; footholds, no Byzantine zeroz

Sublime monotony in Constantinople,
magnificent redundance of red and blue   take me
                                                         back

prolonged formality of degraded systems
reminding us of who we were (and we were)

in original noble design. Once sword
and still. Now sword flung head,
flung head. Now still

red hands in white air knit. Slipped parts of
speech retain and invest their knots. evenness.
                                        evidence.

———	———	———	———
we were	we were	we	were
red hands	white	flung us	parts
———	———	———	———

THE GREAT SYSTEM OF PERFECT COLOR

Blue. Purple. Scarlet deep
with gold [revealed] on [Sinai]
by [GOD] as [noblest]
Others chiefly green
with white & black
used in points of small mass
to relieve blank color

Byzantine flung repetitions

Could we trade length of dress?
Paint unpredicted folds where thigh
opens outward, joints resist
(large blank surfaces)

—four horizontally (lambs,
too) in doorway—noting
nature's tendency
to circle where heat lifts

Gesture of damp gnawing grief

Forgotten twice,
twice refusal of
of ludicrous, cumbrous sheep   grief
sheep leaned as men   gnawing
flocking terminal lines   vertical
Lines, no draperies, broad masses
arm held stiff to pale colors
leaked in vertical bands
Bands continuing,

continuing to

Real faces needed in *the great system of perfect color*,
and different sorts of hair, G. thought

Joachim,

in spite of gold-bordered cape

and halo backdrop returns

empty-handed, marcelled grey hair

(curled rows). Also shepherd's mauve socks

rolled at ankles like us.

White dog jumps up.

No response from Joachim,

e YeSe sidelong.

rounder than

O

His own palpate softens theory's sharp folds

seeing lLargE blank surfaces' close-up seeing

. . . highest strength marked by unconsciousness of its own means of making no small scorn of best result's exertion, intent on other than itself caring little for fruits of each toil (meanwhile "inferior minds intently watching self's process and valuing product's evidence"), there cannot remain the smallest doubt that his mind . . .

        love of beauty   love of truth
entirely free   untinged by
of weakness   severity

industry constant   workmanship
without   accurate
impatience   without formalism

         —John Ruskin's Giotto

----

large blank surfaces

The widows of whiter than butter,

I knew none of them

nor curd's buttery purse nor

shame effect.

Sit away, for instance, to the neck.

In 'here' cathedral's obscure badge.

Rome. 1990

Texts referred to in this work: *Sulla Cappellina degli Scrovegni nell'Arena di Padova,* Sevatico. Padova. 1836. *The Lives of the Artists,* Giorgio Vasari. 1568. (Trans. George Bull. Penguin. New York, 1965.) *Giotto and his Works in Padua,* John Ruskin. London: George Allen. 1905.

when new time folds up

understood and scrupulous

I would have stayed at home as   rehearsal
if a bystander plated in gold,   food
understood and scrupulous among
metal bowls, but a doctor goes
to the Gymnasium where scale is   in key
brick to the heart and air com-
pletely empties itself, without
gender'd regard, thus I tried
my luck as "you," in neutral,
running with you as we talked,
inside the blue grape hyacinth   represses
where nature reproduces its
mechanical force, *rughetta*
wild in tomb grass,

a certain uneven panic

After tomb grass resistance, the occur-
ence of retinal loss, health sections
every Monday yet many coming into focus
of rue, woe, looking sideways, sidereal
normalstrasse, even hearing the gate
bang shut they could not give up where
truck beds beckon, it is such a one in
skirt length, heartbeat crumpled neatly
on white card, leather shoes with-
out pain, your yellow swimsuit dream
pinned on paper head-to-toe, retinal
crosswords, a certain uneven panic in
the presence of marble force, meat's
possible greed,

under us

old movie
dubs

something gray inside of some other gray

A constant construction on the
building's surrounds, high whine
of electric saw on fake marble
under us, something gray inside
of some other gray when work is   digested
going, so I barely notice barking
dogs, very well known people next
to lesser known people, small body
praises Indian broideries, runs
for stethoscope sanction, too late
for champagne, lights turned off
rudely as we look, a wall where   back yards
hangs the triptych typed on a   sanctum
small card,

never sensing her struggle

So that I would rethink, after
my first resistance to my doctor,
never sensing her struggle for
authority, no uniform (like a
New York girls-school-refusal),
lest we get personal and I want
her for my friend but she is my
doctor, irregular and random,
rescuing strict glass cabinets,
neatly typed histories in metal
linguistic purses, preferring her
old Smith-Corona crumpled in a
heap, good prints on walls, our
waiting-room ease,

and all
irritation

a black
shirt with
a black
hat with a
jacket with
black pants

a violated sorted white

Crumpled uniform heap, they shut
the gate before it is not over,
dangling places you've never seen
and could be, similar roses cut,
"his smoothness was a cover-up,"
still rowing in *Wannsee,* bumping
on *Berlinerstrasse,* big room and
wall, a violated sorted white with
tablecloths, a little messy crash,
his wife's instant flash-bulb / bent
paint evidence, the sea could not
keep it out, could not keep the
various gray waves just at the
window out,

whatever
prestige

back of
his
jacket

wet gray slabs against the original

Awakened to car murder noise, will
hit and hit it (siren under hood),
recalcitrant technical murder noise,
boys, TV tennis roar and strut,
my snoring love arise now & go from
sleep's time, cement is grinding and
workers are lobbing wet gray slabs
against the original arch, force
covered and uncovered, disappearing
gelato box, flavors and steam, Anna
in elegant green linen with nothing
in her hands, no mother uniform or
business card, odd hidden welts but
never believing,

repeated
honk

motorino

girlfriend's wheelchair, gathering combs

Panned wide to shut door, soundtrack
gritty, moved camera slowly, returning
tried not to weep while working, denied
all comfort of bread, backward zoom to
youthful self in camp (dream's concen-
tration excrement gone out of control,
skull with your number), wake up,
"Come forward five at a time," a little
speed now, danger over your shoulder, no
eating scenes, girlfriend's wheelchair,
gathering combs, your original murder
plot withdrawn, *"non così, non così"* (not
like that), in white collar, camera
forward, open,

behind
you

Berlinerstrasse
scissors

to be in normal car murder noise

Siren's soundtrack embroideries
have not yet focused the question,
"This key to our apartment . . .
because we were separated . . .
numbers on our skulls . . . will not

shaved
code

be going," (same waltz in 7 / 8 time),
every cut rose, lights above in
air raid position, streaming, now
through *Berlinerstrasse,* in *Wann-*
see I was myself behind a door and
 did not have numbers, compelled to
shower on arrival, aroused from TV
sleep, to be yet here in normal

daylight cement

car murder noise, alive,

no tablecloths, sitting in his car

Rose lights overhead ("I said this
would happen . . . go to Switzerland
where everyone is laughing"), the
reason for war is money or one   not like this
other reason in *rapport,* electric
saw cutting *faux* rose marble floor
importance, waiting for a table to
appear, no tablecloths, sitting in
his car, *gelato* Sunday without   *(non così)*
chairs, establishing radio zone,
clear view from his window, sound
of lover's snore, compressed air,
no *motorino* repairs will pry open
this waking, all pressing,

if brief, my love (my judge)

Cappuccino, *spremuta* at the Bar,
as if this were not car murder war
where we are explosion of plastic
massive force on freeway, we from

                                         value

Palermo, *airportstrasse, autostrada,*
did persist in spite of, wife next
to one's own corpse, decision to
persist, no *kinder* ever, passion

                                 nor children
                                     to him

vigilant, this *amore per la vita,* if
brief, my love (my judge), poured
cement explosion, existing underpass
threatened name's carved stairway
Falcone at our wrist, *egalité,*
ancora, *caffè,*

megaphone whose framework holds air

Deciduous weekday, pantograph map of spring
repeats former leaves and baby speech,
all-new-everything's rebirthed Bar, polished
marble floor, mirror-fronted appliance life,   up
turquoise fake sky on unpacked chairs, secure   scale
and obsessive megaphone whose framework holds
air, the scaffolding's metal habit, turquoise
netting hooked through to nothing, imagined
life in sirens, regulars wait at Bar door
for opening night, or morning, sleeves wait
too, territorial shadow-pack researches   *molto*
tables at *Sergio's,* dividing with certain   *vicino*
justice fresh pizza dough, parceled in air,
slung high . . . and mug beer,

less sinister the plot on film, "unveiled"

Raging dragged child in black-and-white,
part of noise up through scaffolding net,
not seen, soft wet day without windows, the
building sighs, being scraped and drilled,
at every shore some poison leaking, white
tennis shorts, less sinister the plot on   more
film, "unveiled" as if a "neutered thing"
or the absence of no answer, after many
echoing telephone rings, what the others
are doing, one marriage, a baby safely wet
and another yet drying, as if a single day
could affirm our keeping, as if turquoise
chairs and new mirrors might intercede for   contain
what is found,

and caught in rescuing the authority of her task

This almost normal marble day delivers an
urgency in passing—*melone, prosciutto*—and
il dottore does pronounce "a clean slate,"
yet one girl's school refusal, adjusting her
skirt length, replaces glare-free, glassed   soon
certificates for blow-up's ancient broidery,   and late
herself aside big stars in Pleiades (a.k.a.
Seven Sisters, six visible from *Wannsee,* a
seventh "lost"), she wanted me for her friend,
at one moment seeming to be found, but she,
not recognizing this and caught in rescuing   spending
the authority of her task, returned to her
glass cabinet, regularly, randomly glancing
towards the door,

a city's constant and hidden remorse

In the authority of my task, a city's constant
and hidden remorse beneath construction, so that
I would reconsider years of walking *Berliner-*   as
strasse inside air raid siren, early and late   skin
gate's nobility, Keiffer bookshelf scaffolding
and bombed-out paint next to Hannah's red hair
headache, migraine gold angel traveling back-
wards, also *Tempelhof* seen from *der Spargel*
spy tower, & new-leafed dome of synagogue in
gold struck flecky light, so barely noticed
barking dogs returning, jumping recent time,
(it's easy), "But every vein cries out" when   not
new time folds up, in sleep dewy birds never
stop but human song not yet,   singing

Rome-Berlin-Wannsee-Rome
5/4/92–6/9/92
for Hannah Möekel-Rieke

151

New and Uncollected Poems

[Selections from 1978–1995]

1930

Because the shadows are sepia

all the lit precisions seem soft/ a quaking
of leaves that extend their tenuous web
We imagine it gold because it is August

       Marjorie   Ian

eyes averted modestly, so great is their pleasure
in each other

and you see his bare arm, exactly as graceful as
the other young trees   long and willow
compare it

Everywhere, Aspens shiver

the weight of her breasts how the light floats
there

Flowers open because it is summer, their great dark heads lean
into a sexual composure he pretends

against the sapling, seeking balance
in its appearance

while all around them the possibility of doubt hums

wingspans slap and break loose in the hot dust
a tremor behind the leaves

       mother   father

                                        [1978]

A Little Background: the Sisters

Both girls disliked this choosing
warmth

to welcome
each other's manageable oiled silks,

each other's deep water mindfulness,
each semi-

transparent
spread of young espionage.

To one, the mother lay harsher
and larger.

To one,
beneath the brother's husky light

cruel traps of film, wire and color
did elide.

I think I know
(to each she thought) of any woman

lengthened and coiled and
curled.

We are
opaque and cannot know our skin.

We must depend on our gleaming
and bathing,

suddenly complete.
Both girls disliked this equal

sensing of disproportionate
loss,

the tragic
borders of surface and appearance's

blue trap.
This was pain, one said.

I did not grow out of it, and then
I did,

when
the siren pierced me. When

a person bumped the car I
came awake

flaking
scales and fin. I take back

my raised lens. Open. Shut.
Do shed

habit's
childhood, do not tear my hair out

at the bleached roots, do
not pull

the trigger
from a plane above town.

I was my own claustrophobia
climbing

down.
By my brushed plaits

you may have known me. Once.
Once could.

[1987]

"La La at the Cirque Fernando, Paris"

1. La La's recitative

Always Michael,
always
his gold leaf wings about to take off,
but stays,
betting everything
(including me)
from top of granite,
spired closest
to God
(his arch / his angel),
sword above mudflats
or high tide hack
and groan
of blind-handed
water,
feeling all sides of
anything anyone
tries to make hold
to rock—

sucking stone over
stone, flooding
just-broken-bulbs

early March,

early yellow.

•

Michael,
so openly
at your peril,
"our gate to heaven"
my mother said when
I asked,
said he dropped
one night in the dark
inside her, unfolded
his gold wings . . .

and that was enough gold
for me, lacking
father.

.

Just over from the Mont,
Avranches is
where we dragged our sea loot
and sold it on good days.
We'd be hauling and pulling
little live things in shells
from the bay we dug
and he'd glow there, close.

Sundays by boat
or by foot (if sea was down),
two hundred stairs straight up
to the abbey porch, it felt the beginning
and end of praying in my life.

My mom on her knees
on cold granite
asking for the sea to open
plenty for our bucket.

The cathedral light hung
high and lit my body
up as if
it was St. Michael pouring it.
My mother rowed the boat
to get us there. I'll never
forget. Nave and transept filling
with my own spinning silk.

2. Fernando

"Who reads me, when I am ashes,
Is my son in wishes . . ."

It stuck to me, this little promise
dreaming outside the mouth of him
who, singing, wandered lute and throat
in Avranches.
             Walked around sniffing
cheese laid out on the market tables.
Asked "how much," and "how many kinds."
Paid for a branch of plum blossom,
laid it down where I stood.
He was someone traveling
the continent, he said: was Fernando
with his two-handed, one-ring show
and looking for a partner
who wanted to make her own way,
pull silky things
between her legs, furs
in snow.

My mother's eyes went dead.
Spine "soft as cooked apples,"
on her mind. She knew me,
whom I yet did not
know. Knew
to want me = to
her proud, hard rock.

Then he ordered Calvados all around—
for me and my mom, tartes tatin—
and sat near
where we cracked open sea urchins
for lookers to swallow down
whole.

.

(Oh mama, I am your daughter,
in ashes but not in wishes.)

3. La La's song

I could bite down and was strong
and wanted out of that granite place,
she shells always low in the sea mud,
my gaze ever up.

And cells as if by other names did call.
And cells as if by other names did call.

4. The trick

I had Avranches
and St. Michael's unfolding
wings.
FernanDo had a wooden box in a cart,
a ring the size of a wrist,
a pulley, a ship's long rope,
a gear, a handle,
a rubber bit with narrow troughs
for teeth
and a circle he drew with stones.
"The circle's yours,"

he said. "Shut your eyes,.
bite down hard on this
and I'll show you Paris."

He said . . .

but I wasn't listening.
I understood in my teeth.

I said "Begin."

My mouth took
the bit in it. Each time
Fernando turned the handle
he told me to soar like an angel
arching. Going up,
I could see
me spinning from his hand,
taut rope, jawed-down
cells jabbering
rubber bracket bit
& face lifted frown
from my mom pulling mudward,
her tiny grimAce less than shadow.

5. Hearsay

Fernando's talk and Pernod doubles me over
and I'm down. He jams the proprietor
wherever, at the corner bar.

"First saw her little act abroad . . . arched her back
between Calvados and betteRave . . . l'aire du temps!"
                          (black Gauloise air)
"Named her La La, bought her
white gauze, yellow ribbon and
sent her off to the dressmaker for
a seethrough circus suit & a full-length cape
to drop over it . . . or drop to the floor.

"She crosses her ankles when she hangs there
like a bat (a little blind),
twirling

and twirling. Thought

   —Who'd be interested in a naive counTry girl
       just hanging-on with her teeth,
       as if hanging by her neck?—

I'll tell you who."

6. La La's solo

>They said $E = mc^2$
>was there
>like an earring
>setting-off my hair

What color was it? No matter,
some wirey, pulled-back-branching-thing
but I swear (to you) the equation came out of nowhere
and I could be whirRing
in air &

>disappear
>beCalmed
>becoming
>wilderness

>stair

7. Tents

First tent, first show
in gap-tooth townEdge fields of Avranches,
then Coutances, then Caen,
their dense granite particles for eyes
(them eyeing me,
upward-swinging mound of me
wheeling around
as he counted my turns). I counted their
down flung shells of little lunches.

.

"To the tent, gents and. . . ."

.

tent again
rent river
blue cover
bed of snow

　　·

No stopping place, my maiden steerage port-of-aire . . .
I radio dots and dashes from my teeth
to get me through Normandy
(a kind of "prayer" in my mother's country)

　　·

In pain (neck and arms),
but binding myself
with Fernando's words I sink down
between ice and lightning, go inside
of inside (echo & over),
forget to be "me" drifting sugar
in wide bitter sea

　　·

Is shadow
me
in air, in dirt
the same?

Mother,
am I flying?

I think I hear

　　　"hung by the neck" . . .
　　　. . . your chancey stageDoor dare,
　　　　　La La, dear

8. Paris

Suddenly, or is it all along, we're on posters
with our name like other names—*Cirque Fernando*—
& on billets I do exist in the fuzz of someOne's pocket
or am erased or switched from lundi to mercredi,
under presSure.

"Bottoms up, mon cherie!" Fernando says.
(In my dream his cock rises high
with the two-holed snout of a pig. Porc pink.)
"Drink up!" says the boss.

                    •

Fernando's finger rubs Pernod
around
the glass rim
and makes that whining sound
hit air:
"She's long high waves off-balancing incoming tides.
She's skin and ribs with some sort of flying
packed in) (side. To les Halles we row,
a kind of bride for a kind of price.
Not a wren in a cage but nouveau
neck romance, you know?"

                    •

"Ladies and gentlemen: to the tent!"

                    •

So comes that city of papaya ceilings. I row my hair
with arches. Soak in pulp of fruit, go straight up—
my white, cut-out boots laced high over tights.
Let paper faces swalLow me, drink me slowly
from the instant I let the cape fall.

Fernando puts
the bit
between my lips

"and raising her like a cathedral doll
between buttresses, she flies . . ."

(Point of contact)
He says "This is good stuff!"

(between support and thing.)
He yells "La, La, moving you around."

He rubs his hands to flake off light, old dust.
Feels her glow. La La's snow white teeth and
paper money with pretty inked-blue men
again, & again lines his pockets with
The History of Pernod, well-thumbed.

9. Dear Mama,

found my teeth alright
& clamped down.

For strength of molars chewed bark and raw cashews.
But tongue-tied still,
tied down in empty air
with ribbons, yellow, see-through gauze,
(no silky things, no furs)
and more than anything their eyes,
almost always surpRise
when no fall comes.

Fernando's instructions are always
to drop the cape
just as he cranks me up.
(But it's only a cape.)
Inside of inside
I will never drop.

10. The Picture

Found this word *matrix* and its picture:

"any rectangular mathematical arrangement of columns and rows"

a1	b1	c1	d1
a2	b2	c2	d2
a3	b3	c3	d3

and think my only trick was
arranged, but not mathematical

doubling up

as I came down

11. Matrix

a1 Do	b1 Ace	c1 Rave	d1 Try
a2 Ring	b2 Calmed	c2 Edge	d2 Door
a3 One's	b3 Sure	c3 Low	d3 Rise

12. Coda

dear	arc	angel
have	broken	code
now	need	speech

[Mont Saint Michel,
France 2.25.88]

Note: the poem's title is taken from a painting by Edgar Degas (1834–1917), housed in the National Gallery, London.

Fernando's opening couplet, part 2, is quoted from the Preface of Henry Adams' *Mont Saint Michel and Chartres* (Penguin Books, p 5), in which Adams credits its source as simply "Some old Elizabethan play or poem—."

In Commemoration of the Visit of Foreign Commercial Representatives to Japan, 1947

for Bob Glück

Preliminary words

In language, you once hovered. Now you are the hunched body holding the blue oar, so useless in waves. Before I knew your plan, I had already purchased the picture book I called "mine," with its memoir of brown sand extending so casually its territories.

My ignorance in this cannot be excused, yet everything in that room offered itself to me: it was the Foreign Representative who finally caught my eye, between brass hinges. You knew my weakness but sent me there anyway, wanting screens, and you had inscribed the invitation on thick, creamy paper you thought might provide a solution for despair.

Abruptly, just as I stretched out my hand, the mountain presented its snow and deep blue slope, the Foreign Representative's delicate breast. If we can talk about distance, I would propose that series of thatched roofs, the faded hem of the boatman's blue jacket.

Away, my page is one inch longer than at home, with narrower margins; my brush unused, except in commemoration.

I imagine each scratch on the glass pillow to be a person, waiting.

The general headquarters of the allied powers

Beginning from the perspective of the personal, you surprised me with your concrete buddha and dark woolen coats of young European style. How those diminished shadows of trees subtracted us from winter. Badly tinted sky does not represent the "traveler's dream." In your twelve letters, I read a different set of requirements and expectations: our powers linked by windows.

Now our ambitions grow sharper with each darkening rectangle: buildings both dry and thick with steam. Blue water makes its ally with unnatural embankments, yet bodies cling to the edges, and one can see a pair of white trousers in motion, caught with the same swift closure as the black car behind it. I must confess, I had expected the clichés of my childhood and miss them, although I understand your discomfort on hearing this. I draw an ideogram to show you what I mean.

I count on you to translate, as your training requires.

Yomei Mon, the elaborately carved gate of the noted
Tokugawa Shogunate Mausoleum at Nikko, representing
"one of the finest Japanese carvings and lacquer decorations"

What can be represented by this "finest carving" which is too exhaustive to
retain? Our guide has proposed a second look at garish green-and-pink
petals, as if to raise his glass in a toast to our arrival and departure. One
struggles to find words, yet feels the soft diminishing of oxygen. The mon-
umental divests memory of its pockets on foreign soil, where time is a
cloud made solid with carving. I am blinded by my bad faith or lack of ap-
propriate counsel.

Yet this elaboration of gold fell short of sight, as we entered the gate.
Thoughts of death, while normally disturbing, seemed "notable," instead,
as if an excess of enameled color, banded by red, could justify any harsh
loss.

Ashes, scattered on water or under trees, was my family's solution, al-
though now I cannot find my father or my sister and have no specific loca-
tion for my grief. If their ashes and bits of bone were here, in little painted
boxes, would my thoughts arrive in calmer progression?

Japan's "world-famous" Mt. Fuji

One thing appears to be certain. We stand gazing from separate windows in the same hotel. You note the white veins of snow and the pale crusts yet remaining on the near slopes. I think of the Foreign Representative's delicate breast, before confusion came into its dark silk, and economy staged itself, as you might expect, in the popular guises of fame and reform. This drift of quince so close to the hotel window, branching an historical calm—has it changed you into a person someone might banish from sight, for lack of a perfect description? You travel by yellow boat, the April sun is rigorous and punctual; it casts a gloss on every surface, spreading another mountain through the barely moving inches of grey sea. You imagine yourself at diplomatic attention, even choose your trousers and jacket with a longing for precision, while I import a suspect leisure, having served on another occasion.

Now my wish comes and goes with the sun's rigor, expanding and diminishing as if I were one of those white buildings at the foot of the mountain, still read by afternoon light which may fade in an hour, and return.

Ashi-no-ko (Lake Ashi), on the top of Hakone,
a "famous hotspring resort"

Commas, necessarily magnified, curve inside walls, separating rice-paper screens from oxygen. One can consider private matters in silence, give over entirely to the skin's necessity, the water's sulfurous fumes. *A towel, please,* I might have said, if you'd been with me. These learned modesties soon fall before the tremor of red roofs lining the port. The architectural jump creates false pleasure. A colonial banner flaps in the wind like washing hung along the inner court. My tea soothes entirely, in spite of premonitions, and the Foreign Representative tucks the layerings of embroidered silk in the creases of her folded knees and thighs. She hands me the fine-haired brush and a stick of ink, with a little water. I think of drawing you a letter, because words are slipping and faltering under foot. I paint a path of stones which you will recognize, one at a time, as you attempt to extend your influence from those dormer windows, so clearly positioned for their view of flagpoles just at the lake's edge.

Decisions are being taken among the allied powers which, later, will be regretted.

Toro Hatcho, "one of the most picturesque pools in Japan" (Wakayama Prefecture)

I am taken on a boat just wide enough for myself and the boatman, unless we should encounter your party at one of the crossways. Then I would wave to you, hoping to separate you from commerce and modernity, indicating another seat in the boat. Can you feel a drifting like sleep, re-shaping the first idea we were given when they sent us here? While I am not alarmed, I wish to compare these recent days, and the views of water so amply restored to each morning's rising. A certain formality beckons and forbids.

Blue shines up, from between the rafts. I watch the backs of the pole-men pushing their load to the next town. They call out to my boatman, wave a fish and laugh and beckon to us. Their bare toes curve with the wood.

No buildings, for miles now. Only shoals of rock and sharply dropping embankments, leading in no direction I recognize. I look back, thinking of our first meeting and the later dream where you were a woman and I was a man. Now that we have exchanged boundaries and blood types, it is easier. If I do not see you at the impasse, I will understand your message and return to the hotel lobby.

Hirosaki Castle, in northeastern Japan, a "typical citadel" of the feudal lords

"Be a flame for them to pass through," you advised me.

Goju.no.to (five-storied pagoda), in the Kimomizu Dera ("noted Kwannon temple"), in Kyoto, one of the twenty-five sacred temples in Japan

This red will swallow, this temple surround.

Trees lean and persist, worn thin by wind. Bark, leaf and nub salute the small man in gathered cotton trousers with garden shears, now trimming, now bending back a foreign branch. And his father. And his father, before him.

Itsukushima Shrine, in the Inland Sea, "one of the best known scenic spots in Japan"

I've lost sight of where you are journeying, because of the planned charm of "best-known scenery" and weather's unplanned damage to certainty. I could remain here until your return, watching the flicker of silver fins without economic plan or commercial gain. The ordinary is my altar. I think of you holding up your favorite tea-cup, inviting me to commemorate the line of blue hill behind the red gate.

For the first time, I refer to your letter and read your ambivalence, no, your wish to note each change of heart and the substitution of *path* for *daughter,* animal love for speculative representation.

Mt. Zao Skiing Grounds, in northeastern Japan

If white equals mystery and snow equals death, how am I to understand the two bent figures in black on the ski slope? I choose the one with his shadow intact and hope that it's you, for lack of binoculars. Your form appears admirable and the shadow to your right, entirely severed and autonomous except at the feet. From this perspective, a diagonal gash of blue sky gives geometric relief to a moment so perfectly caught it might slip into fiction. I could "go on" about the snow-covered trees but decisions are hovering like already memorized language. You are needed by the allied powers who require your shadow ability. I'm tapping the air between us and hoping you can hear me. Do not depend on the former treaty or visual aids. Here is the list you sent me:

> *"rough, smooth, dark, blond, rich, middle class, tender, cruel, narcissist, altruist, east, west"*

No one is "alike," and neither are you, though joined at the feet with your daytime abilities.

Daibutsu, in Kamakura, the giant bronze Buddha image, rising forty feet high

I think that SCALE must be the shadow of domination. I cannot look. (Or is it, *You don't want to.*)

Arashiyama, in Kyoto, noted for its cherry blossoms
and autumn leaves

Again, the human. A silly heart for Sunday—today, hands inside of hands, the procession of covered boats rocking from side-to-side in their slow pace down the river. Your "daughter" holding her paper parasol painted with falcons and Lily wagging her tail and limping along the left bank of the Arashiyama, flowing over—almost—with melted snow . . . such patient and difficult lovers.

You leap to the boat, a little drunk, and I am your ally in pines and grilled sea bass. I have not booked the return trip due to a seasonal error. The errand you sent me on, also the Foreign Representative arriving for tea and the multiple bodies of water in my life are discrete but not conclusive arrangements. What was once a refusal lingers, as if pine needles had broken and spread their scent on the skin—a new ideogram I am trying to paint, whenever I lift my brush.

Nijubashi, the "famous double arch bridge, the gateway" to the Imperial Palace

Tunneling forward towards the awaited arch at the opposite end, the mind *does* see, then the eye—following yearning—grabs hold of space and watches it expand until the curved frame is lost, the opening regained.

We observe the double arch of Nijubashi through this split-second lens so that reflections of imperial design may curve and flash as if we were looking for ourselves in the moving plaits of water, the solidity of human desire all equal and held intact for our reference and imagined stability. How tiny we are, seen from there. How calm, the unsevered branches of silver and green, the lush and edible yellow fruit of the ginkgos about to pierce their coverings and burst through.

Because we opened the same book, we are bound by these ties of silk, particularly at the gateway.

[May, 1988]

Cue or Starting Point

BIRD

Sometimes they fly in pairs   about the length of one
                                                            window

Sometimes they are ponderous   as big blades and
windowshades over grass

brown paper is to brown field algebraic   as if one

but not the other one gives up
being alike   pointing at something obvious

BIRD

t d k and s often carry us
emerge outside of
ending us
as swallows rush

and Vespas tear over   long plastic strips of
                                                  blue and yellow
                                                        binding
                                                      brake and

break free of us
birds know the length of us even
from behind a window and look down

                                                        in that
                              brown black sketchbook ordering

wing   wind how made

TREE

"the thing about trees is . . .   relentlessly
                                                        consistent" antennae

untenable metal staple
yet flies down silvery night each length   of bee wing

                                            rung after rung, dark's light
                                    it perched on pieces of blue cloth

CLOUD

Arm in arm, across tarmac   pointing her to

thin coral cloud stream   (pious in
                                                                reproduction)

above piazza's ancient fruit tints   (tropical flush in
                                            some other island context)

"I think it means rain"   (wrong, again)

late March, knowing she needed to see this emptiness, clouds and the one
tree (which didn't leaf out) gone

TREE

One did hear   the flow of nearby branches
shear occasional and limp

yet this rawness   moves, is
                                                                     moving
even sudden atrophy   of limb

BIRD

see an emptiness shoot off
                              narrow path stapled with wing lengths
dependent on scale, your under-
                                     estimation of how it could
eat at you, that movement
                                          (left behind itself)

BIRD

not a protective   thing   but the negative
incision not brown   field   of scissor
cut   wing   right up
                                                    against it

looked downward & saw one long pointing & another up

to remove it
paint between sound   scratchy big stillness
of birds
and other inward flutter   still did not move

CLOUD

My hands had to move as fast as the Vespa over tarmac

Clouds drew themselves   No it was some ordering
principle pulling or pushing   it was the sketch-

book's empty page and the little box of staples

                          Something shining outside the black line
not finished

---

for Sanda Iliescu, after her drawings/notation
Rome.May/1995

WING

I. THE UNDERDRAWINGS

The New comes forward in its edges in order to be itself;

its volume by necessity becomes violent and three-dimensional
and ordinary, all similar models shaken off and smudged

as if memory were an expensive thick creamy paper and every
corner turned now in partial erasure,

even bits of pearly rubber, matchstick and lucent plastic
leaving traces of decision and little tasks performed

as if each dream or occasion of pain had tried to lift itself
entirely away, contributing to other corners, planes and
accumulated depth

.

the wing is not static but frayed, layered, fettered, furling and
stony

its feathers cut as if from tissue or stiffened cheesecloth
condensed in preparation for years of stagework

attached to its historic tendons; more elaborate
the expansive ribcage, grieving, stressed, yet

marked midway along the breastbone with grains of light

.

there are two men, they are tall men, and they are talking softly
among the disintegrating cubes

A cube's clean volume
its daily burnt mark
backwards into match
day's oxygen, common
the remaining light
nothing changed yet
have a way of crash

through matter heart
are two men turning
that one particular
to unfold in expand
stars: "that which
improvised on deep
picking, pecking at
sent to tell us what

shatters and reassembles
the New is used and goes
sticks one struck at each
pinched breath and nerve
bricked-up Now melt with
he persists as does pain
ing in on you, swimming

rate in each cell There
their limit of blanket
evening appears in reds
ing brilliant traces or
is known to us" or just
kitchen floor meanwhile
our skins ghost or angel
we didn't want to know

It can happen that the intoxicating wing will draw the mind as a
bow   The cubic route of wing falls backwards with light
leaking through at the edge   The cube is formally particular
and a part of speech and lost   it looks for like kind,
regardless of function, and attempts to replace itself   The
square root of anything captures and holds, seeming to be final,
and we are grateful   We see the delicate marks along the
feather and we follow, now to define or depict the outskirts of
meaning   A plume of smoke or any of the growths which cover
the bodies of birds   To form a model of the wing's surface,
the cube arrives on a day called "the darkest day"   Its
likeness consists of strength, atonality, pigment, emptiness and
shafts partly hollow   I put my mouth just at the opening where
a steel edge gives way to an angle   from which light emerges
along its soft narrow barbs   If the wing had a voice it would
open through a shaft   *I am not of that feather*

IV. LINE

Attached by some "natural" substance
the arm (or leg) with elbow

(or joint) midway suggests the next
incision or protrusion: It stiffens as

a fin or rib projecting new function:

It emits signals periscopic (familiar)
helical into the spinal: Wing

could loosen that line's identity calling
to itself with charcoal error

"only in contradiction to that which is known
to us of nature"

Even the New is attached or marked by attachment

the shimmer of wing, which claim may tell us everything
in a white blink

just as in troubled moments it disappears

> [A young girl in Arkansas, the quill of an angel in
> warm light, from orange and yellow regions, falls]

Waking touched

> [an angel stands in technicolor as cosmonauts look out
> on   Jet-liner wingspan   attaching itself collectively]

these retinal bodies larger, remarkable for their iridescence

He extends thus into plumage as fruit rubbed from walls soaks
inward

.

Your mango human skin doth beckon overlaps against the larger
screen

.

Where floods our night hike, features of body assemble
their hawkeyed distance

abnormally retaining jet-liner lure

.

yet wanting the same thing always: your innocence
dressed in red anterior borders

pinion and spur, my teeth which may fit the angel's gear

.

having seen thy ancient ground

messenger : *ἀγγελος* : wing

now and melt with rush all   in one place nothing changed   I
did not grow up I   went away in one phase   brooded I over
skier   in black the flyer, forces   that dive far yet he
persists   in contradiction to   as does physical pain
that which is known a way   of crashing in on you   to us
changing, now perilous   their spots unawares your own
heart stopping   she used words downward   who like
brilliance   but are you turning   he had no truck with the
mysterious   like stones found   not having opened after
each other, Herodotus   the sifted swimming through matter
cocoa color   I was thought though burning   hot except
our gills' events   but where his cold hand   did not flow
touched   a normal one throwing   up screens & satisfied
lest they be struggling   with his dictum and   bickering
plain as   the palm on a particular   evening to attract
brilliant treads   something more with a cleft on its   upper
lip appearing   to unfold as if marked

as does that
which is of
crashing to
us changing
their spots   aware your own she
heart stop   she used words like
downward who   brilliance turning
but are you   he had in my hand

swimming through
color, I was burn
hot gills' events   struggling
cold hand touched   dictum and
                      plain as
                      a particular
                      attraction
                      treads some
                      thing cleft
                      if marked

IX. MATTER

There are two men without feet, they are tall men swimming through matter.

forward edge itself to be volume by necessity as if partial
edge itself to be volume by necessity as if partial erase
itself to be volume by necessity as if partial erase
to be volume by necessity as if partial erase
be volume by necessity as if partial erase
volume by necessity as if partial erase
by necessity as if partial erase
necessity as if partial erase
as if partial erase
if partial erase
partial erase
erase
of
pearly
lucent
decision
and
little
tasks
of
pain
had
tried
to
lift
to lift
tried to lift
had tried to lift
pain had tried to lift
of pain had tried to lift
tasks of pain had tried to lift
little tasks of pain had tried to lift
and little tasks of pain had tried to lift
decision and little tasks of pain had tried to lift
lucent decision and little tasks of pain had tried to lift

erase
other
corners
planes
accumulate
depth
condensed
in
preparation
stagework
historic
tendons
elaborate
ribcage
marked
midway
with
grains
of
light
talking
softly
among
disintegrating
cubes
the
falling
wing
will
draw
the
mind
as
a
bow

itself   the   wing   not   static   but   frayed,   layered,   fettered,   furling

Notes on Poems

"Magritte Series" was originally published as Number 6 in the first pamphlet series from Tuumba Press, 1977 (edited by Lyn Hejinian). The poems were written ten years after seeing the major Magritte retrospective at the Museum of Modern Art in New York in the mid-1960s with Frank O'Hara, who had curated the show.

"re:searches" was written in Rome during the aftermath of the Chernobyl accident, when radioactive clouds endangered grazing lands (and thus milk supplies) as they blew across Europe. Concurrent with this event was the "fallout" from reading Anakreon's fragments (translated by Guy Davenport) and Susan Howe's *My Emily Dickinson,*—understanding that Dickinson's words had been mutilated and censored by her brother, literally scissored out of letters she'd written to her woman friend (his wife) . . . that in fragment lay potency.

"Etruscan Pages" was written in May/June of 1991, after a pilgrimage to Etruscan burial sites scattered over the Maremma coast north of Rome. During the period of the poem's writing, I was further informed by dreams, as well as by archeological texts assembled by King Gustave Adolf of Sweden from an Etruscan dig he'd organized in 1962. Materials from these sources—and from the Villa Giulia in Rome—were incorporated into the poem's evolving form, as were phrases (in quotes) from D. H. Lawrence's essay "Etruscan Places," marking recognition of sensations we shared, but substituting *page* for *place.* My worry that Lawrence might have said it all soon vanished as I saw (during an intentional rereading of his essay, after completing several drafts of my poem), that he'd never been to Norchia, where my most vivid experience had unfolded . . . still, I wanted to trade notes with him. Also, reading an early draft of Rachel Blau DuPlessis's 1979 essay "For the Etruscans" undoubtedly inscribed another dimension of cultural loss that I would not fully take in until standing among the empty cliff tombs and, later, in front of the hand-incised names of the dead cut into stones preserved by museums yet bearing very little text to translate.

"Giotto : ARENA" Reading critical assessments of a "master," after being in the actual presence of Giotto's work; understanding from Ruskin and Vasari that Giotto's ongoing friendship with Dante involved painting the very same neighbors into Arena Chapel frescoes as those being written into Dante's *In-*

ferno. Wanting to foreground the meanings inherent in "faulty copying" (as typos visualize them); playing error against mastery—the fixed Byzantine model of "perfection" as tripped-up by Giotto's break from type.

"when new time folds up" was written through months of exterior reconstruction and modernization of the nineteenth-century *condominio* where I live in Rome, after post-Wall deconstruction in Berlin/Wannsee (and feeling the pulse of neo-Naziism gathering just under Berlin's surface during a trip there); and after reentry into Italy the day Judge Falcone—with his wife and another colleague—were blown up by the Mafia on the Palermo autostrada. The 13 1/2-line "sonnets" are meant to explode bits of matter into the right margin.

"In Commemoration of the Visit of Foreign Commercial Representatives to Japan, 1947" is based on a small book of picture postcards assembled as a memento of Japan's finest tourist sites, to be given to their new allies (and recent adversaries). I discovered the book when my friend Bob Glück sent me to an Asian antique store, where he thought I might find "little things" for Christmas gifts. Seeing the postcard book in the $1 box, I bought a copy for each of us and began to write a poem sequence based on each of the photos and their captions. Not knowing my plan, he did the same.

"La La at the Cirque Fernando, Paris" discovered its final matrix of words inside the existing partial draft of the poem, arising initially from a typo only noticed in the retyping of part 4, in which the <u>D</u> in the second syllable of Fernan<u>D</u>o had been accidentally capitalized. La La's grid of words was <u>then</u> constructed from the second parts of other two-syllable words, searched out in the already existing text; La La's private matrix thus evolves from her own fragmented story— that of a young circus performer, learning to hang by her teeth from a ring. Within minutes the matrix appeared, revealing a core lexicon or set of word clues needed by La La in order for her to come into possession of her own voice and her autonomy from "the boss." The "Coda" followed swiftly.

"Cue or Starting Point" was stimulated by Sanda Iliescu's "drawings," constructed entirely with staples and strips of plastic, exhibited in the American Academy of Rome annual spring exhibit of artists in residence, 1995.

"WING" was suggested by Mel Bochner's *Drawings* (David Nolan Gallery, NYC, 1988) and by Bochner's 1993 installation *Via Tasso* at the Museo Storico della Liberazione di Roma; Jess's "paste-up" (cover for Norma Cole's *Mars*) delivered my point of focus for entering and retrieving certain materials of the poem. "WING" was dedicated to the memory of Joe Brainard, who died of AIDS during its writing, and to his companion, the poet and librettist Kenward Elmslie, who has kept the spirit of reinvented language alive.

Author's Afterword

> "It would exist but I could never touch it again. I had
> made it. I had gone beyond my inside and forgotten it.
> There it stands. And sometimes still I am among the for-
> merly mine, find myself there adrift and obscure. Turn-
> ing and turning from these pages."
> —Clark Coolidge, *The Book of During*

Shaping a *Selected Poems* is, in part, a fictional process in which the history of one's
passage from silence into language makes its claim in *impure* ways. The artifact—
that version of "poem" finally let go into print—never really attains a static resting
place, and now the truth of restlessness is reengaged. All one has sought to learn
in this continuous apprenticeship asserts itself and wants, yet again, to rewrite it-
self (to incarnate) so as to incorporate new information. But the event of the origi-
nal writing retains its own authority and temporal moment, its *making* often hav-
ing been determined as much by unplanned "accident"—covert error leading to
unimpeded risk—as by the peculiar emotional resonance or formal design ini-
tially intended. Isn't the typo, after all, a word trying to escape its single-version
identity? It wants deciphering. Just as the alphabet is "at large," so is the fugitive
identity of the poem . . . on the prowl, looking for its next escape from the already
known.

How, then, to construct a path or *oeuvre*, looking backward over twenty-five
years of writing? When last heard from, the identified writer, with her percep-
tions and aesthetic ideas seemingly intact, has been altered by each random or de-
liberate encounter: a particular accountability again reconstructs itself via intrigue
of syntactic pressure and visual/aural event. Subtraction, multiplication, fleeting
cognition. This opening of the manifold has been the lure from the beginning . . .
and whatever fragment hovers just beyond the constructed border, what Basil
Bunting once called "that which approximates most clearly the linguistic event."
The sub-lingua tilts into motions of writing.

Turning to these pages, gazing at "the formerly mine," making and remaking
my choices, some poems have continued to emit a powerful contact, still breath-
ing in me. Others rest or resist, calm or squirming in their moment. In the early
part of this process, I asked trusted writer-friends to read and to cull judiciously
from my first cut. Although none got their way entirely, due to inevitable aes-
thetic differences and space limitations, I am deeply grateful to those first read-

ers—Susan Gevirtz, Myung Mi Kim, Peter Weltner, and Robert Glück. Mary Margaret Sloan's close reading provided the final ferocity, at that stage . . . and certain reclamations, for which I am particularly beholden. Each reader brought a unique and necessary perspective to my final decisions, and was generous with his or her time.

Coming somewhat later in this process and furthering its completion with humor and generous critical advice were Peter and Meredith Quartermain. My thanks, also, to Nick Piombino and Burton Hatlen, who originally (and separately) put it into my head to collect/select from a life's work and place it between covers. My special gratitude, also, to Brenda Hillman, whose very thoughtful reading of my work, as well as her timely comments, helped steer me toward Wesleyan.

To my editors, Suzanna Tamminen, who discreetly guided this manuscript through various unrehearsed stages with remarkable lucidity and the ready curiosity of a true reader, and Eileen McWilliam, its initial navigator/protector, and to the poets chosen as outside readers, my deeply felt thanks for that often unremarked and unrewarded belief in the work—the book—that supports, definitively, the poet's vulnerable journey from private utterance to public text.

For artistic and critical support, I have been fortunate in the additional friendships of my sister Anne Bagwell, JoAnn Ugolini and Don Cushman, Norma Cole, Ellen Dissanyake, Sujenna Anderson, Irene Skolnick, Frances Jaffer, Carolyn Burke, Rachel Blau DuPlessis, Marjorie Perloff, Mei-mei Berssenbrugge, and Emily Barton . . . and grateful to my scholar friends and translators in Italy, Annalisa Goldoni, Marina Morbiducci, Marina Camboni, Toni Maraini, Alberto Rossatti, Franco LaPolla, and Giuseppe Caputo.

Especial ongoing love and esteem for my husband, Arthur Bierman, who has believed in my work and supported me at each step of its completion; in particular, I am grateful for his visual sensitivity and unflagging intellectual curiosity.

Finally, I pay homage to those writers who, living during my lifetime, have provided me with particular and lasting ways of paying attention to the word's mystery and exact turning: Wallace Stevens, Marianne Moore, H.D., Lorine Niedecker, Louis Zukofsky, George Oppen, Charles Olson, Robert Creeley, Frank O'Hara, Barbara Guest, James Schuyler, Joseph Ceravolo, Jack Spicer and Basil Bunting . . . and to those many trusting, scrappy, fantastically talented students who took a chance with me, extending their knowledge and mine, to willingly push their poetic limits.

UNIVERSITY PRESS OF NEW ENGLAND publishes books under its own imprint and is the publisher for Brandeis University Press, Dartmouth College, Middlebury College Press, University of New Hampshire, Tufts University, and Wesleyan University Press.

ABOUT THE AUTHOR

Kathleen Fraser is the author of fourteen books of poetry, including most recently *WING* (Em Press, 1995), *when new time folds up* (Chax Press, 1993), and *boundayr* (The Lapis Press, 1987). She published and edited the feminist/experimentalist poetry journal *HOW(ever)* and from 1972–1992 was professor of Creative Writing at San Francisco State University.

LIBRARY OF CONGRESS CATALOGING-IN-PUBLICATION DATA

Fraser, Kathleen, 1937–

Il cuore : the heart : selected poems, 1970–1995 / Kathleen Fraser.

   p.   cm. — (Wesleyan poetry)

   ISBN 0–8195–2244–9 (alk. paper). — ISBN 0–8195–2245–7 (pbk. : alk. paper)

   I. Title. II. Series

PS3556.R353C86   1997   97–23564

811´.54—DC21